SECOND EDITION

Simple Program Design

a step by step approach

SECOND EDITION

Simple Program Design

Lesley Anne Robertson

Course Technology, Inc. One Main Street, Cambridge, MA 02142

Nelson   I(T)P®
102 Dodds Street
South Melbourne 3205

Simultaneously published by Course Technology, Inc
One Main Street
Cambridge, MA 02142

Nelson   I(T)P® *an International Thomson Publishing company*

First published in 1993
10 9 8 7
05 04 03 02 01 00 99 98 97
Copyright © Lesley Anne Robertson

Nelson   I(T)P® edition ISBN 0 17 08822 7

National Library of Australia
Cataloguing-in-Publication data

Robertson, Lesley Anne.
    ISBN 0 17 008822 7.
    Simple program design.
    2nd ed.
    1. Programming (Electronic computers). 2. Structured programming.
    3. Pseudocode (Computer program language). I. Title.
005.12

Boyd & Fraser edition ISBN 0-87709-283-4

Cover designed by David Albon
Text designed by Christina Neri
Printed by L. Rex Printing Co. Ltd.

Nelson Australia Pty Limited ACN 004 603 454 (incorporated in
Victoria) trading as Nelson ITP.

Contents

4   Selection control structures

Expands the selection control structure by introducing multiple selection, nested selection, and the case construct in pseudocode. Several algorithms, using variations of the selection control structure, are developed.

5   Repetition control structures

Develops algorithms which use the repetition control structure in the form of DOWHILE, REPEAT...UNTIL, and counted repetition loops.

6   Pseudocode algorithms using sequence, selection and repetition

Develops algorithms to eight simple programming problems using combinations of sequence, selection and repetition constructs. Each problem is properly defined; the control structures required are established; a pseudocode algorithm is developed; and the solution is manually checked for logic errors.

7   Modularisation

Introduces modularisation as a means of dividing a problem into subtasks. Hierarchy charts are introduced as a pictorial representation of program module structure. Several algorithms which use a modular structure are developed.

8 Communication between modules

Defines elementary data items and data structures and introduces the concepts of inter-module communication, local and global data, and the passing of parameters between modules. Algorithms which pass parameters are developed. The concept of object-oriented design is introduced, and the terms associated with it are defined.

9 Cohesion and coupling

Introduces the concepts of module cohesion and coupling. Several levels of cohesion and coupling are described, and pseudocode examples of each level are provided.

10 General pseudocode algorithms for common business problems

Develops a general pseudocode algorithm for five common business applications. All problems are defined; a hierarchy chart is established; and a pseudocode algorithm is developed, using a mainline and several subordinate modules. The topics covered include report generation with page break, a single-level control break, a multiple-level control break, a sequential file update program, and array processing.

11 Conclusion

A revision of the steps involved in good program design.

Appendix 1 Nassi-Schneiderman diagrams

Covers Nassi-Schneiderman diagrams for those students who prefer a more diagrammatic approach to program design. Algorithms which use a combination of sequence, selection and repetition constructs are developed in some detail.

Appendix 2 Special algorithms

Contains a number of algorithms which are not included in the body of the book but may be required at some time in a programmer's career.

Preface

With the increased popularity of programming courses in our universities, colleges and technical institutions, there is a need for an easy-to-read textbook on computer program design. There are already dozens of introductory programming texts using specific languages such as PASCAL, BASIC, COBOL or C, but they usually gloss over the important step of designing a solution to a given programming problem.

This textbook tackles the subject of program design by using structured programming techniques and pseudocode to develop a solution algorithm. The recommended pseudocode has been chosen because of its closeness to written English, its versatility and ease of manipulation, and its similarity to the syntax of most structured programming languages.

Simple Program Design is designed for programmers who want to develop good programming skills for solving common business problems. Too often, programmers who are faced with a problem launch straight into the code of their chosen programming language, instead of concentrating on the actual problem at hand. They become bogged down with the syntax and format of the language, and often spend many hours getting the program to work. Using this textbook, the programmer will learn how to define the problem, how to design a solution algorithm, and how to prove the algorithm's correctness, before coding a single statement from any programming language. By using pseudocode and structured programming techniques, the programmer can concentrate on developing a well-designed and correct solution, and thus eliminate many frustrating hours at the testing phase.

The book is divided into eleven chapters, beginning with a basic explanation of structured programming techniques, top-down development and modular design. Then, concept by concept, the student is introduced to the syntax of pseudocode; methods of defining the problem; the application of basic control structures in the development of the solution algorithm; desk checking techniques; hierarchy charts; module design; parameter passing; object-oriented design methodology; and many common algorithms.

Each chapter thoroughly covers the topic at hand, giving practical examples relating to business applications, and a consistently structured approach when representing algorithms and hierarchy charts.

This second edition of *Simple Program Design* contains material which is an extension to that in the first edition. Nassi-Schneiderman (N-S) diagrams have been removed from the body of the book and are introduced and developed entirely in Appendix 1. Appendix 1 has been written for those programmers who prefer a more diagrammatic approach to algorithm design and solutions to all the pseudocode algorithms in Chapters 2, 3, 4 and 5 have been presented again in this appendix using N-S diagrams.

This second edition also contains a number of early examples and problems which do not involve file processing. Because the examples are interactive, many of them can be coded directly into a programming language, and executed, before the topic of file processing has been covered.

The concepts of arrays and parameter passing are introduced early in the book, with many examples provided. Object-oriented design methodology and information hiding are introduced in Chapter 8, and dynamic data structures such as queues, stacks and linked lists are introduced in Appendix 2.

I would like to thank Dr Malcolm Cook at the University of Western Sydney for his suggestions and assistance with this second edition; my husband, David, for editing the manuscript; and my brother, Rick Noble, for his amusing cartoons.

Lesley Anne Robertson

Program design

STEPS IN PROGRAM DEVELOPMENT

Computer programming is an art. Many people believe that a programmer must be good at mathematics, have a memory for figures and technical information, and be prepared to spend many hours sitting at a terminal, typing programs. However, given the right tools, and steps to follow, anyone can write well-designed programs. It is a task worth doing, as it is both stimulating and fulfilling.

Programming can be defined as the development of a solution to an identified problem, and the setting up of a related series of instructions which, when directed through computer hardware, will produce the desired results. It is the first part of this definition which satisfies the programmer's creative needs: that is, to design a solution to an identified problem. Yet this step is so often overlooked. Leaping straight into the coding phase without first designing a proper solution usually results in programs that contain a lot of errors. Often the programmer needs to spend a significant amount of time finding these errors and correcting them. A more experienced programmer will design a solution to the program first, desk check this solution, and then code the program in a chosen programming language.

There are seven basic steps in the development of a program. An outline of these seven steps follows.

1   Define the problem

This step involves carefully reading and rereading the problem until you understand completely what is required. To help with this initial analysis, the problem should be divided into three separate components:

- the inputs,
- the outputs, and
- the processing steps to produce the required outputs.

A defining diagram as described in Chapter 3 is recommended in this analysis phase, as it helps to separate and define the three components.

2   Outline the solution

Once the problem has been defined, you may decide to break the problem up into smaller tasks or steps, and establish an outline solution. This initial outline is usually a rough draft of the solution which may include:

- the major processing steps involved,
- the major subtasks (if any),
- the major control structures (e.g. repetition loops),
- the major variables and record structures, and
- the mainline logic.

The solution outline may also include a hierarchy or structure chart. The steps involved in creating this outline solution are detailed in Chapters 2 to 6.

3 Develop the outline into an algorithm

The solution outline developed in Step 2 is then expanded into an algorithm: a set of precise steps which describe exactly the tasks to be performed and the order in which they are to be carried out. This book uses pseudocode (a form of structured English) to represent the solution algorithm, as well as structured programming techniques. Nassi-Schneiderman diagrams are also provided in Appendix 1 for those who prefer a more pictorial method of algorithm representation. Algorithms using pseudocode and the Structure Theorem are developed thoroughly in Chapters 2 to 6.

4 Test the algorithm for correctness

This step is one of the most important in the development of a program, and yet it is the step most often forgotten. The main purpose of desk checking the algorithm is to identify major logic errors early, so that they may be easily corrected. Test data needs to be walked through each step in the algorithm to check that the instructions described in the algorithm will actually do what they are supposed to. The programmer walks through the logic of the algorithm, exactly as a computer would, keeping track of all major variables on a sheet of paper. Chapter 3 recommends the use of a desk check table to desk check the algorithm, and many examples of its use are provided.

5 Code the algorithm into a specific programming language

Only after all design considerations have been met in the previous four steps should you actually start to code the program into your chosen programming language.

6 Run the program on the computer

This step uses a program compiler and programmer-designed test data to machine-test the code for both syntax and logic errors. This is usually the most rewarding step in the program development process. If the program has been well designed then the usual time-wasting frustration and despair often associated with program testing are reduced to a minimum. This step may need to be performed several times until you are satisfied that the program is running as required.

7   Document and maintain the program

Program documentation should not be listed as the last step in the program development process, as it is really an ongoing task from the initial definition of the problem to the final test result.

Documentation involves both external documentation (such as hierarchy charts, the solution algorithm, and test data results) and internal documentation which may have been coded in the program. Program maintenance refers to changes which may need to be made to a program throughout its life. Often these changes are performed by a different programmer from the one who initially wrote the program. If the program has been well designed using structured programming techniques, the code will be seen as self documenting, resulting in easier maintenance.

1.2   STRUCTURED PROGRAMMING

Structured programming helps you to write effective, error-free programs. The original concept of structured programming was set out in a paper published in 1964 in Italy by Bohm and Jacopini. They established the idea of designing programs using a Structure Theorem based on three control structures. Since then a number of authors, such as Edsger Dijkstra, Niklaus Wirth, Ed Yourdon and Michael Jackson, have developed the concept further and have contributed to the establishment of the popular term 'structured programming'. This term now refers not only to the Structure Theorem itself, but also to top-down development and modular design.

Top-down development

Traditionally, programmers presented with a programming problem would start coding at the beginning of the problem and work systematically through each step until reaching the end. Often they would get bogged down in the intricacies of a particular part of the problem, rather than considering the solution as a whole. In the top-down development of a program design, a general solution to the problem is outlined first. This is then broken down gradually into more detailed steps until finally the most detailed levels have been completed. It is only after this process of 'functional decomposition' (or 'stepwise refinement') that the programmer starts to code. The result of this systematic, disciplined approach to program design is a higher precision of programming than was possible before.

Modular design

Structured programming also incorporates the concept of modular design, which involves grouping tasks together because they all perform the same function (e.g. calculating sales tax or printing report headings). Modular design is connected directly to top-down development, as the steps or subtasks into which the programmer breaks up the program solution will actually form the future modules of the program. Good modular design aids in the reading and understanding of the program.

The Structure Theorem

The Structure Theorem revolutionised program design by eliminating the GOTO statement and establishing a structured framework for representing the solution. The theorem states that it is possible to write any computer program by using only three basic control structures. These control structures are:

- sequence;
- selection, or IF-THEN-ELSE; and
- repetition, or DOWHILE.

They are covered in detail in Chapter 2.

1.3   AN INTRODUCTION TO ALGORITHMS AND PSEUDOCODE

Structured programming techniques require a program to be properly designed before coding begins, and it is this design process which results in the construction of an algorithm.

What is an algorithm?

An algorithm is like a recipe: it lists the steps involved in accomplishing a task. It can be defined in programming terms as a set of detailed, unambiguous and ordered instructions developed to describe the processes necessary to produce the desired output from a given input. The algorithm is written in simple English and is not a formal document. However, to be useful, there are some principles which should be adhered to. An algorithm must:

- be lucid, precise and unambiguous;
- give the correct solution in all cases; and
- eventually end.

For example, if you want to instruct someone to add up a list of prices on a pocket calculator, you might write an algorithm like the following:

Turn on calculator
Clear calculator

Repeat the following instructions
    Key in dollar amount
    Key in decimal point (.)
    Key in cents amount
    Press addition (+) key
Until all prices have been entered

Write down total price
Turn off calculator

Notice that in this algorithm the first two steps are performed once, before the repetitive process of entering the prices. After all the prices have been entered and summed, the total price can be written down and the calculator can be turned off. These final two activities are also performed only once. This algorithm satisfies the desired list of properties: it lists all the steps in the correct order from top to bottom, in a definite and unambiguous fashion, until a correct solution is reached. Notice that the steps to be repeated (entering and summing the prices) are indented, both to separate them from those steps performed only once and to emphasise the repetitive nature of their action. It is important to use indentation when writing solution algorithms because it helps to differentiate between the three control structures.

What is pseudocode?

Flowcharts were once used to represent the steps in an algorithm diagrammatically, but they were bulky and difficult to draw, and often led to poor program structure. In contrast, pseudocode is easy to read and write, as it represents the statements of an algorithm in English. Pseudocode is really structured English. It is English which has been formalised and abbreviated to look very like high-level computer languages.

There is no standard pseudocode at present. Authors seem to adopt their own special techniques and sets of rules, which often resemble a particular programming language. This book attempts to establish a standard pseudocode for use by all programmers, regardless of the programming language they choose. Like many versions of pseudocode, this version has certain conventions, as follows:

1   Statements are written in simple English.
2   Each instruction is written on a separate line.
3   Keywords and indentation are used to signify particular control structures.

4   Each set of instructions is written from top to bottom, with only one
    entry and one exit.
5   Groups of statements may be formed into modules, and that group given
    a name.

Pseudocode has been chosen to represent the solution algorithms in this
book because its use allows the programmer to concentrate on the logic of the
problem.

An alternative pictorial method of representing algorithms using Nassi-
Schneiderman diagrams is described in detail in Appendix 1.

1.4   CHAPTER SUMMARY

In this chapter, the steps in program development were introduced and
briefly described. These seven steps are:

1   Define the problem.
2   Outline the solution.
3   Develop the outline into an algorithm.
4   Test the algorithm for correctness.
5   Code the algorithm into a specific programming language.
6   Run the program on the computer.
7   Document and maintain the program.

Structured programming was presented as a combination of three separate
concepts: top-down development, modular design, and the use of the
Structure Theorem when designing a solution to a problem.

An algorithm was defined as a set of detailed, unambiguous and ordered
instructions developed to describe the processes necessary to produce the
desired output from the given input. Pseudocode is an English-like way of
representing the algorithm; its advantages and some conventions for its use
were listed.

Pseudocode

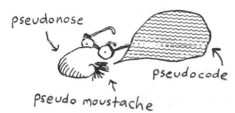

pseudonose

pseudocode

pseudo moustache

HOW TO WRITE PSEUDOCODE

When designing a solution algorithm, you need to keep in mind that the set of instructions written will eventually be performed by a computer. That is, if you use words and phrases in the pseudocode which are in line with basic computer operations, the translation from the pseudocode algorithm to a specific programming language becomes quite simple.

This chapter establishes six basic computer operations and introduces common words and keywords used to represent these operations in pseudocode. Each operation can be represented as a straightforward English instruction, with keywords and indentation to signify a particular control structure.

Six basic computer operations

1   A computer can receive information

When a computer is required to receive information or input from a particular source, whether it be a terminal, a disk or any other device, the verbs Read and Get are used in pseudocode. Read is usually used when the algorithm is to receive input from a record on a file, while Get is used when the algorithm is to receive input from the keyboard. For example, typical pseudocode instructions to receive information are:

```
Read student name
Get system date
Read number_1, number_2
Get tax_code
```

Each example uses a single verb, Read or Get, followed by one or more nouns to indicate what data is to be obtained. At no stage is it necessary to specify the source of the data, as this information is not required until run time.

2   A computer can put out information

When a computer is required to supply information or output to a device, the verbs Print, Write, Put, Output or Display are used in pseudocode. Print is usually used when the output is to be sent to the printer, while Write is used when the output is to be written to a file. If the output is to be written to the screen, the words Put, Output or Display are used in pseudocode. Typical pseudocode examples are:

```
Print 'Program Completed'
Write customer record to master file
Put out name, address and postcode
Output total_tax
Display 'End of data'
```

In each example, the data to be put out is described concisely using mostly lower-case letters.

3 A computer can perform arithmetic

Most programs require the computer to perform some sort of mathematical calculation, or formula, and for these, a programmer may use either actual mathematical symbols or the words for those symbols. For instance, the same pseudocode instruction can be expressed as either of the following:

```
Add number to total
total = total + number
```

Both expressions clearly instruct the computer to add one value to another, so either is acceptable in pseudocode. The equal symbol, =, has been used to indicate assignment of a value as a result of some processing.

To be consistent with high-level programming languages, the following symbols can be written in pseudocode:

+ for Add
− for Subtract
* for Multiply
/ for Divide
() for Brackets

The verbs Compute and Calculate are also available. Some pseudocode examples to perform a calculation are:

```
Divide total_marks by student_count
sales_tax = cost_price * 0.10
Compute C = (F − 32) * 5/9
```

4 A computer can assign a value to a piece of data

There are three cases where you may write pseudocode to assign a value to a piece of data:

1 To give data an initial value in pseudocode, the verbs Initialise or Set are used.
2 To assign a value as a result of some processing, the symbol '=' is written.
3 To keep a piece of information for later use, the verbs Save or Store are used.

Some typical pseudocode examples are:

```
Initialise total accumulators to zero
Set student_count to 0
total_price = cost_price + sales_tax
Store customer_num in last_customer_num
```

5   A computer can compare two pieces of information and select one of two alternative actions

An important computer operation available to the programmer is the ability to compare two pieces of information and then, as a result of the comparison, select one of two alternative actions. To represent this operation in pseudocode, special keywords are used: IF, THEN, and ELSE. The comparison of data is established in the IF clause, and the choice of alternatives is determined by the THEN or ELSE options. Only one of these alternatives will be performed. A typical pseudocode example to illustrate this operation is:

```
IF student is part_time THEN
     add 1 to part_time_count
ELSE
     add 1 to full_time_count
ENDIF
```

In this example the attendance status of the student is investigated, with the result that either the part_time_count or the full_time_count accumulator is incremented. Note the use of indentation to emphasise the THEN and ELSE options, and the use of the delimiter ENDIF to close the operation.

6   A computer can repeat a group of actions

When there is a sequence of processing steps which need to be repeated, two special keywords, DOWHILE and ENDDO, are used in pseudocode. The condition for the repetition of a group of actions is established in the DOWHILE clause, and the actions to be repeated are listed beneath it. For example:

```
DOWHILE student_total < 50
     Read student record
     Print student name, address to report
     Add 1 to student_total
ENDDO
```

In this example it is easy to see the statements which are to be repeated, as they immediately follow the DOWHILE statement and are indented for added emphasis. The condition which controls and eventually terminates the repetition is established in the DOWHILE clause, and the keyword ENDDO acts as a delimiter. As soon as the condition for repetition is found to be false, control passes to the next statement after the ENDDO.

Some teachers of PASCAL as a first programming language prefer to use the keywords WHILE...DO and ENDWHILE to start and end this operation, as follows:

```
WHILE student_total < 50 DO
    Read student record
    Print student name, address to report
    Add 1 to student_total
ENDWHILE
```

Note that the format, indentation and operation of DOWHILE and WHILE...DO are exactly the same. The only difference is the actual keywords which are used.

2.2 THE STRUCTURE THEOREM

The Structure Theorem forms the basic framework for structured programming. It states that it is possible to write any computer program by using only three basic control structures that are easily represented in pseudocode: sequence, selection, and repetition.

The three basic control structures

1 Sequence

The sequence control structure is the straightforward execution of one processing step after another. In pseudocode we represent this construct as a sequence of pseudocode statements.

```
statement a
statement b
statement c
```

The sequence control structure can be used to represent the first four basic computer operations listed previously: to receive information, put out information, perform arithmetic, and assign values. For example, a typical sequence of statements in an algorithm might read:

```
Add 1 to page_count
Print heading line
Set linecount to zero
Read customer record
```

These instructions illustrate the sequence control structure as a straightforward list of steps written one after the other, in a top-to-bottom fashion. Each instruction will be executed in the order in which it appears.

2   Selection

The selection control structure is the presentation of a condition and the choice between two actions, the choice depending on whether the condition is true or false. This construct represents the decision making abilities of the computer and is used to illustrate the fifth basic computer operation, namely to compare two pieces of information and select one of two alternate actions.

In pseudocode, selection is represented by the keywords IF, THEN, ELSE and ENDIF:

```
IF condition p is true THEN
      statement(s) in true case
ELSE
      statement(s) in false case
ENDIF
```

If condition p is true then the statement or statements in the true case will be executed, and the statements in the false case will be skipped. Otherwise (the ELSE statement) the statements in the true case will be skipped and statements in the false case will be executed. In either case, control then passes to the next processing step after the delimiter ENDIF. A typical pseudocode example might read:

```
IF student is part_time THEN
      add 1 to part_time_count
ELSE
      add 1 to full_time_count
ENDIF
```

A variation of the selection control structure is the null ELSE structure, which is used when a task is performed only if a particular condition is true. The null ELSE construct is written in pseudocode as:

```
IF condition p is true THEN
      statement(s) in true case
ENDIF
```

Note that the keyword ELSE is omitted. This construct tests the condition in the IF clause and, if that is found to be true, performs the statement or statements listed in the THEN clause. However, if the initial condition is found to be false, then no action will be taken and processing will proceed to the next statement after the ENDIF.

3   Repetition

The repetition control structure can be defined as the presentation of a set of instructions to be performed repeatedly, as long as a condition is true. The basic idea of repetitive code is that a block of statements is executed again and again, until a terminating condition occurs. This construct represents the sixth basic computer operation, namely to repeat a group of actions. It is written in pseudocode as:

```
DOWHILE condition p is true
      statement block
ENDDO
```

The DOWHILE loop is a leading decision loop; that is, the condition is tested before any statements are executed. If the condition in the DOWHILE statement is found to be true, the block of statements following that statement is executed once. The delimiter ENDDO then triggers a return of control to the retesting of the condition. If the condition is still true the statements are repeated, and so the repetition process continues until the condition is found to be false. Control then passes to the statement which follows the ENDDO statement. It is imperative that at least one statement within the statement block can alter the condition and eventually render it false, because otherwise the logic may result in an endless loop.

The DOWHILE statement could also have been written as a WHILE...DO statement using exactly the same format, indentation and operation, as follows:

```
WHILE condition p is true DO
      statement block
ENDWHILE
```

Here is a pseudocode example which represents the repetition control structure:

```
Set student_total to zero
DOWHILE student_total < 50
      Read student record
      Print student name, address to report
      Add 1 to student_total
ENDDO
```

This example illustrates a number of points:

1   The variable student_total is initialised before the DOWHILE condition is executed.
2   As long as student_total is less than 50 (i.e. the DOWHILE condition is true), the statement block will be repeated.
3   Each time the statement block is executed, one instruction within that block will cause the variable student_total to be incremented.
4   After 50 iterations, student_total will equal 50, which causes the DOWHILE condition to become false and the repetition to cease.

It is important to realise that the initialising and subsequent incrementing of the variable tested in the condition is an essential feature of the DOWHILE construct.

2.3 CHAPTER SUMMARY

In this chapter, six basic computer operations were listed, along with pseudocode words and keywords to represent them. These operations were: to receive information, put out information, perform arithmetic, assign a value to a piece of data, decide between two alternate actions, and repeat a group of actions. Typical pseudocode examples were given as illustrations.

The Structure Theorem was introduced. It states that it is possible to write any computer program by using only three basic control structures: sequence, selection, and repetition. Each control structure was defined, and its association with each of the six basic computer operations was indicated. Pseudocode examples for each control structure were provided.

Developing an algorithm

3.1 DEFINING THE PROBLEM

Chapter 1 described seven steps in the development of a computer program. The very first step, and one of the most important, is defining the problem. This involves carefully reading and rereading the problem until you understand completely what is required. Quite often, additional information will need to be sought to help resolve any ambiguities or deficiencies in the problem specifications. To help with this initial analysis, the problem should be divided into three separate components:

1   Input: a list of the source data provided to the problem.
2   Output: a list of the outputs required.
3   Processing: a list of actions needed to produce the required outputs.

When reading the problem statement, the input and output components are easily identified, because they use descriptive words such as nouns and adjectives. The processing component is also identified easily. The problem statement usually describes the processing steps as actions, using verbs and adverbs.

When dividing a problem into its three different components, you should simply analyse the actual words used in the specification, and divide them into those which are descriptive and those which imply actions. It may help to underline the nouns, adjectives, and verbs and verb parts used in the specification.

In some programming problems, the inputs, processes and outputs may not be clearly defined. In such cases it is best to concentrate on the outputs required. Doing this will then decide most inputs, and the way will then be set for determining the processing steps required to produce the desired output.

At this stage the processing section should be a list of what actions need to be performed, not how they will be accomplished. Do not attempt to find a solution until the problem has been completely defined. Let's look at a simple example.

EXAMPLE 3.1   *Add three numbers*

A program is required to read three numbers, add them together, and print their total.

Tackle this problem in two stages. Firstly, underline the nouns and adjectives used in the specification. This will establish the input and output components as well as any objects which are required. With the nouns and adjectives underlined, our example would look like this:

A program is required to read three numbers, add them together, and print their total.

By looking at the underlined nouns and adjectives you can see that the input for this problem is three numbers and the output is the total. It is helpful to write down these first two components in a simple diagram, called a defining diagram.

Input	Processing	Output
number_1 number_2 number_3		total

Secondly, underline (in a different colour) the verbs and adverbs used in the specification. This will establish the actions required. Example 3.1 should now look like this:

A program is required to <u>read</u> three numbers, <u>add</u> them <u>together</u>, and <u>print</u> their total.

By looking at the underlined words, it can be seen that the processing verbs are read, add together and print. These steps can now be added to our defining diagram to make it complete. Note that when writing down each processing verb, the objects or nouns associated with each verb should also be included. The defining diagram now becomes:

Input	Processing	Output
number_1 number_2 number_3	Read three numbers Add numbers together Print total number	total

Now that all the nouns and verbs in the specification have been considered and the defining diagram is complete, the problem has been properly defined. That is, we now understand the input to the problem, the output to be produced, and the processing steps required to convert the input to the output.

Meaningful names

At this stage in defining the problem it is a good idea to introduce some unique names which will be used to represent the variables or objects in the problem and to describe the processing steps. All names should be meaningful. A name given to a variable is simply a method of identifying a particular storage location in the computer.

The uniqueness of the name will differentiate it from other locations. Often a name describes the type of data stored in a particular variable. For instance, a variable may be one of the three simple data types, namely an integer, a real number or a character. The name itself should be transparent enough to adequately describe the variable: number_1, number_2 and number_3 are more meaningful names for three numbers than A, B and C.

When it comes to writing down the processing component of the defining diagram, you should use words which describe the work to be done in terms of single, specific tasks or functions. In Example 3.1 the processing steps would be written down as verbs accompanied by their associated objects:

```
Read three numbers
Add numbers together
Print total number
```

There is a pattern in the words chosen to describe these steps. Each action is described as a single verb followed by a two-word object. Studies have shown that if you follow this convention to describe a processing step, two benefits result. Firstly, you are using a disciplined approach to defining the problem; secondly, the processing is being dissected into separate tasks or functions. This simple operation of dividing a problem into separate functions and choosing a proper name for each function is extremely important later, when considering modules.

EXAMPLE 3.2   *Find average temperature*

A program is required to prompt the terminal operator for the maximum and minimum temperature readings on a particular day, accept those readings as integers, and calculate and display to the screen the simple average temperature, calculated by (maximum temperature + minimum temperature) / 2.

First establish the input and output components by underlining the nouns and adjectives in the problem statement.

A program is required to prompt the terminal operator for the maximum and minimum temperature readings on a particular day, accept those readings as integers, and calculate and display to the screen the simple average temperature, calculated by (maximum temperature + minimum temperature) / 2.

The input component is the maximum and minimum temperature readings and the output is the average temperature. Using meaningful names, these components can be set up in a defining diagram as follows:

Input	Processing	Output
max_temp		avg_temp
min_temp		

Now establish the processing steps by underlining the verbs in the problem statement.

A program is required to <u>prompt</u> the terminal operator for the maximum and minimum temperature readings on a particular day, <u>accept</u> those readings as integers, and <u>calculate</u> and <u>display</u> to the screen the simple average temperature, calculated by (maximum temperature + minimum temperature) / 2.

The processing verbs are prompt, accept, calculate and display. By finding the associated objects of these verbs, the defining diagram can now be completed, as follows:

Input	Processing	Output
max_temp min_temp	Prompt for temperatures Get max, min temperatures Calculate average temperature Display average temperature	avg_temp

Remember that at this stage you are only concerned with the fact that the simple average temperature must be calculated, not how the calculation will be performed. That will come later, when the solution algorithm is established.

EXAMPLE 3.3 *Compute mowing time*

A program is required to read in the <u>length</u> and <u>width</u> of a rectangular house block, and the <u>length</u> and <u>width</u> of the rectangular house which has been built on the block. The algorithm should then compute and display the <u>time</u> required to cut the grass around the house, at the rate of two square metres per minute.

To establish the input and output components in this problem, the nouns or objects have been underlined. By reading these words, it can be seen that the input is the length and width of the block, and the length and width of the house. The output is the time to cut the grass.

The input and output components can be set up in a defining diagram, as follows:

Input	Processing	Output
block_length block_width house_length house_width		mowing_time

Now the verbs and adverbs in the problem statement can be underlined.

A program is required to <u>read</u> in the length and width of a rectangular house block, and the length and width of the rectangular house which has been built on the block. The algorithm should then <u>compute</u> and <u>display</u> the time required to cut the grass around the house, at the rate of two square metres per minute.

The processing steps can now be added to the defining diagram:

Input	Processing	Output
block_length	Prompt for block measurements	mowing_time
block_width	Get block measurements	
house_length	Prompt for house measurements	
house_width	Get house measurements	
	Calculate mowing area	
	Calculate mowing time	

These steps are sufficient to establish the requirements of the problem. You must be absolutely confident of what is to be done in the program before you attempt to establish how it is done.

3.2   DESIGNING A SOLUTION ALGORITHM

Designing a solution algorithm is the most challenging task in the life cycle of a program. Once the program has been properly defined, you usually begin with a rough sketch of the steps required to solve the problem. Look at what is required and, using these requirements and the three basic control structures defined in the Structure Theorem, attempt to establish how the processing will take place.

The first attempt at designing a particular algorithm usually does not result in a finished product. Steps may be left out, or some that are included may later be altered or deleted. Pseudocode is useful in this trial and error process, since it is relatively easy to add, delete, or alter an instruction. Do not hesitate to alter algorithms, or even discard one and start again, if you are not completely satisfied with it. If the algorithm is not correct, then the program will never be.

There is some argument that the work of a programmer ends with the algorithm design. After that, a coder or trainee programmer could take over and code the solution algorithm into a specific programming language. In practice, this usually doesn't happen. However, it is important that you not be too anxious to start coding until the necessary steps of defining the problem and designing the solution algorithm have been completed.

Here are solution algorithms for the preceding three examples. All involve sequence control structures only; there are no decisions or loops, and so, the solution algorithms are relatively simple.

EXAMPLE 3.4 *Solution algorithm for Example 3.1*

A program is required to read three numbers, add them together and print their total.

A Defining diagram

Input	Processing	Output
number_1	Read three numbers	total
number_2	Add numbers together	
number_3	Print total number	

This diagram shows what is required, and a simple calculation will establish how. Using pseudocode, and the sequence control structure, the solution algorithm can be established as follows:

B Solution algorithm

```
Add_three_numbers
    Read number_1, number_2, number_3
    total = number_1 + number_2 + number_3
    Print total
END
```

There are a number of points to consider in this solution algorithm:

1 A name has been given to the algorithm, namely Add_three_numbers. Names should briefly describe the function of the algorithm, and are usually expressed as a single verb followed by a two-word object. Other names which are equally suitable include Process_three_numbers and Total_three_numbers.

2 An END statement at the end of the algorithm indicates that the algorithm is complete.

3 All processing steps between the algorithm name and the END statement have been indented for readability.

4 Each processing step in the defining diagram relates directly to one or more statements in the algorithm. For instance, 'Read three numbers' in the defining diagram becomes 'Read number_1, number_2, number_3' in the algorithm; and 'Add numbers together' becomes 'total = number_1 + number_2 + number_3'.

Now that the algorithm is complete, you should desk check the solution and then translate it into a programming language. (Desk checking is covered in Section 3.3.)

EXAMPLE 3.5   *Solution algorithm for Example 3.2*

A program is required to prompt the terminal operator for the maximum and minimum temperature readings on a particular day, accept those readings as integers, and calculate and display to the screen the simple average temperature, calculated by (maximum temperature + minimum temperature) / 2.

A   *Defining diagram*

Input	Processing	Output
max_temp	Prompt for temperatures	avg_temp
min_temp	Get max, min temperatures	
	Calculate average temperature	
	Display average temperature	

Using pseudocode, a simple calculation and the sequence control structure, the algorithm can be expressed as follows:

B   *Solution algorithm*

```
Find_average_temperature
    Prompt operator for max_temp, min_temp
    Get max_temp, min_temp
    avg_temp = (max_temp + min_temp) / 2
    Output avg_temp to the screen
END
```

In this example the step 'Calculate average temperature' in the defining diagram has been expressed in the algorithm as actual calculations to compute and display the average temperature.

EXAMPLE 3.6   *Solution algorithm for Example 3.3*

A program is required to read in the length and width of a rectangular house block, and the length and width of the rectangular house which has been built on the block. The algorithm should then compute and display the time required to cut the grass around the house, at the rate of two square metres per minute.

A Defining diagram

Input	Processing	Output
block_length	Prompt for block measurements	mowing_time
block_width	Get block measurements	
house_length	Prompt for house measurements	
house_width	Get house measurements	
	Calculate mowing area	
	Calculate mowing time	

The actions to be carried out in this algorithm are listed sequentially in the processing component of the defining diagram. At this stage the processing steps still only describe the steps to be performed, in their correct order. Meaningful names such as block_length and mowing_time have been given to the variables within the algorithm for readability.

B The solution algorithm

```
Calculate_mowing_time
      Prompt operator for block_length, block_width
      Get block_length, block_width
      block_area = block_length * block_width
      Prompt operator for house_length, house_width
      Get house_length, house_width
      house_area = house_length * house_width
      mowing_area = block_area - house_area
      mowing_time = mowing_area / 2
      Output mowing_time to screen
END
```

3.3 CHECKING THE SOLUTION ALGORITHM

After a solution algorithm has been constructed it must be tested for correctness. This step is necessary, because most major logic errors occur during the development of the algorithm, and if not detected, these errors would be passed on to the program. It is much easier to detect errors in pseudocode than in the corresponding program code. This is because once programming begins, you usually assume that the logic of the algorithm is correct. Then, when errors are detected, your attention is focused on the individual lines of code to identify the problems rather than the initial logic expressed in the algorithm. It is often too difficult to step back and analyse the program as a whole. As a result, many frustrating hours can be wasted during testing, which could have been avoided by just five minutes spent desk checking the solution algorithm.

Desk checking involves tracing through the logic of the algorithm with some chosen test data. That is, you walk through the logic of the algorithm exactly as a computer would, keeping track of all major variable values on a sheet of paper. This playing computer not only helps to detect errors early, but also helps you become familiar with the way the program runs. The closer you are to the execution of the program, the easier it is to detect errors.

Selecting test data

When selecting test data to desk check an algorithm, you must look at the program specification and choose simple test cases only, based on the requirements of the specification, not the algorithm. By doing this you will still be able to concentrate on what the program is supposed to do, not how.

To desk check the algorithm, you need only a few simple test cases which will follow the major paths of the algorithm logic. A much more comprehensive test will be performed once the algorithm has been coded into a programming language.

Steps in desk checking an algorithm

There are six simple steps to follow when desk checking an algorithm:

1 Choose simple input test cases which are valid. Two or three test cases are usually sufficient.
2 Establish what the expected result should be for each test case. This is one of the reasons for choosing simple test data in the first place: it is much easier to determine the total of 10, 20 and 30 than 3.75, 2.89 and 5.31!
3 Make a table of the relevant variable names within the algorithm on a piece of paper.
4 Walk the first test case through the algorithm, keeping a step-by-step record of the contents of each variable in the table as the data passes through the logic.
5 Repeat the walk-through process using the other test data cases, until the algorithm has reached its logical end.
6 Check that the expected result established in Step 2 matches the actual result developed in Step 5.

By desk checking an algorithm you are attempting to detect early errors. Desk checking will eliminate most errors, but it still cannot prove that the algorithm is 100% correct!

Now let us desk check each of the algorithms developed in this chapter:

EXAMPLE 3.7 *Desk check of Example 3.1*

A *Solution algorithm*

```
Add_three_numbers
    Read number_1, number_2, number_3
    total - number_1 + number_2 + number_3
    Print total
END
```

B *Desk checking*

(i) Choose two sets of input test data. The three numbers selected will be 10, 20, and 30 for the first test case and 40, 41, and 42 for the second.
Input data:

	First data set	Second data set
number_1	10	40
number_2	20	41
number_3	30	42

(ii) Establish the expected result for each test case.
Expected results:

	First data set	Second data set
total	60	123

(iii) Set up a table of relevant variable names, and pass each test data set through the solution algorithm, statement by statement.

Statement		number_1	number_2	number_3	total	Print
First Pass	Read	10	20	30		
	total				60	
	Print					yes
Second Pass	Read	40	41	42		
	total				123	
	Print					yes

(iv) Check that the expected results (60 and 123) match the actual results (the total column in the table).

This desk check, which should take no more than five minutes, indicates that the algorithm is correct. You can now proceed to code the algorithm into a programming language.

EXAMPLE 3.8   *Desk check of Example 3.2*

A   Solution algorithm

```
Find_average_temperature
    Prompt operator for max_temp, min_temp
    Get max_temp, min_temp
    avg_temp = (max_temp + min_temp) / 2
    Output avg_temp to the screen
END
```

B   Desk checking

(i) Choose two sets of input test data. The max_temp and min_temp values will be 30 and 10 for the first case, and 40 and 20 for the second.
Input data:

	First data set	Second data set
max_temp	30	40
min_temp	10	20

(ii) Establish the expected result for each test case.
Expected results:

	First data set	Second data set
avg_temp	20	30

(iii) Set up a table of variable names, and pass each test data set through the solution algorithm, statement by statement.

Statement		prompt	max_temp	min_temp	avg_temp	Output
First Pass	Prompt	yes				
	Get		30	10		
	Calculate				20	
	Output					yes
Second Pass	Prompt	yes				
	Get		40	20		
	Calculate				30	
	Output					yes

(iv) Check that the expected results in step (ii) match the actual results in step (iii).

EXAMPLE 3.9   *Desk check of Example 3.3*

A   *Solution algorithm*

```
Calculate_mowing_time
    Prompt operator for block_length, block_width
    Get block_length, block_width
    block_area = block_length * block_width
    Prompt operator for house_length, house_width
    Get house_length, house_width
    house_area = house_length * house_width
    mowing_area = block_area – house_area
    mowing_time = mowing_area / 2
    Output mowing_time to screen
END
```

B   *Desk checking*

(1) Choose two sets of valid input data. The data chosen will be as illustrated in the diagram.

Input data:

	First data set	Second data set
block_length	30	40
block_width	30	20
house_length	20	20
house_width	20	10

(ii) Expected results:

	First data set	Second data set
mowing_time	250 minutes	300 minutes

(iii) Set up a table of variable names and pass each test data set through the solution algorithm, statement by statement.

Statement	block length	block width	house length	house width	block area	house area	mowing area	mowing time
First Pass								
Get	30	30						
block_area					900			
Get			20	20				
house_area						400		
mowing_area							500	
mowing_time								250
Output								yes
Second Pass								
Get	40	20						
block_area					800			
Get			20	10				
house_area						200		
mowing_area							600	
mowing_time								300
Output								yes

(iv) Check that the expected results match the actual results.

Yes, the expect result for each set of data matches the calculated result.

3.4   CHAPTER SUMMARY

The first section of this chapter was devoted to methods of analysing and defining a programming problem. You must fully understand a problem before you can attempt to find a solution. The method suggested was to analyse the actual words used in the specification with the aim of dividing the problem into three separate components: input, output and processing. Several examples were explored and the use of a defining diagram was established. It was emphasised that the processing steps should list what tasks need to be performed, rather than how they are to be accomplished.

The second section was devoted to the establishment of a solution algorithm. After the initial analysis of the problem you must attempt to find a solution and express this solution as an algorithm. To do this you must use correct pseudocode statements, the three basic control structures, and the defining diagram which had previously been established. Only algorithms using the sequence control structure were used as examples.

The third section was concerned with checking the algorithm for correctness. A method of playing computer by tracing through the algorithm step by step was introduced, with examples to previous problems given.

3.5   PROGRAMMING PROBLEMS

In the following problems you will need to:

- define the problem by constructing a defining diagram,
- create a solution algorithm using pseudocode, and
- desk check the solution algorithm using two valid test cases.

1   Construct an algorithm which will prompt an operator to input three characters, receive those three characters, and display a welcoming message to the screen such as 'Hello xxx! We hope you have a nice day'.

2   A program is required which will receive two integer items from a terminal operator, and display to the screen their sum, difference, product and quotient.

3   A program is required which will read in a tax rate (as a percentage) and the prices of five items. The program is to calculate the total price, before tax, of the items and then the tax payable on those items. The tax payable is computed by applying the tax rate percentage to the total price. Both values are to be printed as output.

4   A program is required to read in one customer's account balance at the beginning of the month, a total of all withdrawals for the month, and a total of all deposits made during the month. A federal tax charge of 1% is applied to all transactions made during the month. The program is to calculate the account balance at the end of the month by (1) subtracting the total withdrawals, (2) adding the total deposits, and (3) subtracting the federal tax, from the account balance at the beginning of the month. After calculation, the balance at the end of the month is to be printed.

5   A program is required which will read in the values from an employee's time sheet, and calculate and print the weekly pay owing to that employee. The values read in are the total number of regular hours worked, the total overtime hours, and the hourly wage rate. Payment for regular hours worked is to be computed as rate times hours; payment for overtime hours is to be computed at time-and-a-half. Weekly pay is calculated as payments for regular hours worked, plus payment for overtime hours worked.

Selection control structures

THE SELECTION CONTROL STRUCTURE

The selection control structure was introduced in Chapter 2, as the second construct in the Structure Theorem. This structure represents the decision-making capabilities of the computer. That is, you can use the selection control structure in pseudocode to illustrate a choice between two or more actions, depending on whether a condition is true or false. There are a number of variations of the selection structure, as follows.

1 Simple selection (simple IF statement)

Simple selection occurs when a choice is made between two alternative paths, depending on the result of a condition being true or false. The structure is represented in pseudocode using the keywords IF, THEN, ELSE and ENDIF. For example:

```
IF account_balance < $300 THEN
    service_charge = $5.00
ELSE
    service_charge = $2.00
ENDIF
```

Only one of the THEN or ELSE paths will be followed, depending on the result of the condition in the IF clause.

2 Simple selection with null false branch (null ELSE statement)

The null ELSE structure is a variation of the simple IF structure. It is used when a task is performed only when a particular condition is true. If the condition is false, then no processing will take place and the IF statement will be bypassed. For example:

```
IF student_attendance = part_time THEN
    add 1 to part_time_count
ENDIF
```

In this case, the part_time_count field will be altered only if the student's attendance pattern is part time.

3 Combined selection (combined IF statement)

A combined IF statement is one which contains multiple conditions, each connected with the logical operators AND or OR. If the conditions are combined using the connector AND, then both conditions must be true for the combined condition to be true. For example:

```
IF  student_attendance = part_time
AND student_gender = female THEN
    add 1 to fem_part_time_count
ENDIF
```

In this case, each student record will undergo two tests. Only those students who are female and who attend part time will be selected, and the variable fem_part_time_count will be incremented. If either condition is found to be false, then the counter will remain unchanged.

If the connector OR is used to combine any two conditions, then only one of the conditions needs to be true for the combined condition to be considered true. If neither condition is true, then the combined condition is considered false. Changing the AND in the above example to OR dramatically changes the outcome from the processing of the IF statement.

```
IF student_attendance = part_time
OR student_gender = female THEN
    add 1 to fem_part_time_count
ENDIF
```

In this example, if either or both conditions is found to be true, then the combined condition will be considered true. That is, the counter will be incremented:

1   if the student is part time, regardless of gender; or
2   if the student is female, regardless of attendance pattern.

Only students who are not female and not part time will be ignored. So fem_part_time_count will contain the total count of female part-time students, male part-time students, and female full-time students. As a result, fem_part_time_count is no longer a meaningful name for this variable. You must fully understand the processing which takes place when combining conditions with the AND or OR logical operators.

More than two conditions can be linked together with the AND or OR operators. However, if both operators are used in the one IF statement, brackets must be used to avoid ambiguity. Look at the following example:

```
IF  record_code = '23'
OR  update_code = delete
AND account_balance = zero THEN
    delete customer record
ENDIF
```

The logic of this statement is confusing. It is uncertain whether the first two conditions should be grouped together and operated on first, or the second two conditions should be grouped together and operated on first. Pseudocode algorithms should never be ambiguous. There are no precedence rules for logical operators in pseudocode, so brackets must be used to explicitly state the intended order of processing as follows:

```
IF  (record_code = '23'
OR  update_code = delete)
AND account_balance = zero THEN
     delete customer record
ENDIF
```

4   Nested selection (nested IF statement)

Nested selection occurs when the word IF appears more than once within an IF statement. Nested IF statements can be classified as linear or non-linear.

Linear nested IF statements

The linear nested IF statement is used when a field is being tested for various values and a different action is to be taken for each value.

This form of nested IF is called linear because each ELSE immediately follows the IF condition to which it corresponds. Comparisons are made until a true condition is encountered, and the specified action is executed until the next ELSE statement is reached. Linear nested IF statements should be indented for readability, with each IF, ELSE and corresponding ENDIF aligned. For example:

```
IF record_code = 'A' THEN
    increment counter_A
ELSE
    IF record_code = 'B' THEN
        increment counter_B
    ELSE
        IF record_code = 'C' THEN
            increment counter_C
        ELSE
            increment error_counter
        ENDIF
    ENDIF
ENDIF
```

Note that there are an equal number of IF, ELSE and ENDIF statements, and that the correct indentation makes it easy to read and understand.

Non-linear nested IF statements

A non-linear nested IF occurs when a number of different conditions need to be satisfied before a particular action can occur. It is termed non-linear because the ELSE statement may be separated from the IF statement with which it is paired. Indentation is once again important when expressing this form of selection in pseudocode. Each ELSE statement should be aligned with the IF condition to which it corresponds.

For instance:

```
IF student_attendance = part_time THEN
    IF student_gender = female THEN
        IF student_age > 21 THEN
            add 1 to mature_fem_pt_students
        ELSE
            add 1 to young_fem_pt_students
        ENDIF
    ELSE
        add 1 to male_pt_students
    ENDIF
ELSE
    add 1 to full_time_students
ENDIF
```

Note that there are an equal number of IF conditions as ELSE and ENDIF statements. Using correct indentation helps to see which pair of IF and ELSE statements match. However, non-linear nested IF statements may contain logic errors which could be difficult to correct, so they should be used sparingly in pseudocode. If possible, replace a series of non-linear nested IF statements with a combined IF statement. This replacement is possible in pseudocode because two consecutive IF statements act like a combined IF statement which uses the AND operator. Take as an example the following non-linear nested IF statement:

```
IF student_attendance = part_time THEN
    IF student_age > 21 THEN
        increment mature_pt_student
    ENDIF
ENDIF
```

This can be written as a combined IF statement:

```
IF student_attendance = part_time
AND student_age > 21 THEN
    increment mature_pt_student
ENDIF
```

The same outcome will occur for both pseudocode expressions, but the format of the latter is preferred, if the logic allows it, simply because it is easier to understand.

4.2 ALGORITHMS USING SELECTION

Let us look at some programming examples which use the selection control structure. In each example, the problem will be defined, a solution algorithm will be developed and the algorithm will be manually tested. To help define the problem, the processing verbs in each example have been underlined.

EXAMPLE 4.1   *Read three characters*

Design an algorithm which will:
prompt a terminal operator for three characters, accept those characters as
input, sort them into ascending sequence and output them to the screen.

A   *Defining diagram*

Input	Processing	Output
char_1	Prompt for characters	char_1
char_2	Accept three characters	char_2
char_3	Sort three characters	char_3
	Output three characters	

B   *Solution algorithm*

The solution algorithm requires a series of IF statements to sort the three
characters into ascending sequence.

```
Read_three_characters
     Prompt the operator for char_1, char_2, char_3
     Get char_1, char_2, char_3
     IF char_1 > char_2 THEN
          temp = char_1
          char_1 = char_2
          char_2 = temp
     ENDIF
     IF char_2 > char_3 THEN
          temp = char_2
          char_2 = char_3
          char_3 = temp
     ENDIF
     IF char_1 > char_2 THEN
          temp = char_1
          char_1 = char_2
          char_2 = temp
     ENDIF
     Output to the screen char_1, char_2, char_3
   END
```

In this solution, most of the logic of the algorithm is concerned with the
sorting of the three characters into alphabetic sequence. To make the
algorithm easier to read, this sorting logic could have been performed in a
single module, as will be demonstrated in Chapter 7.

C Desk checking

Two sets of valid characters will be used to check the algorithm; the characters k, b and g as the first set, and z, s and a as the second.

(i) Input data:

	First data set	Second data set
char_1	k	z
char_2	b	s
char_3	g	a

(ii) Expected results:

	First data set	Second data set
char_1	b	a
char_2	g	s
char_3	k	z

(iii) Desk check table:

Note that when desk checking the logic, each IF statement is treated as a single statement.

Statement		char_1	char_2	char_3	temp	IF statement executed?
First Pass	Get	k	b	g		
	IF	b	k		k	yes
	IF		g	k	k	yes
	IF					no
	output	yes	yes	yes		
Second Pass	Get	z	s	a		
	IF	s	z		z	yes
	IF		a	z	z	yes
	IF	a	s		s	yes
	output	yes	yes		yes	

EXAMPLE 4.2 *Process customer record*

A program is required to <u>read</u> a customer's name, a purchase amount and a tax code. The tax code has been validated and will be one of the following:

0   tax exempt (0%)
1   state sales tax only (3%)
2   federal and state sales tax (5%)
3   special sales tax (7%)

The program must then <u>compute</u> the sales tax and the total amount due and <u>print</u> the customer's name, purchase amount, sales tax and total amount due.

A Defining diagram

Input	Processing	Output
cust_name	Read customer details	cust_name
purch_amt	Compute sales tax	purch_amt
tax_code	Compute total amount	sales_tax
	Print customer details	total_amt

B Solution algorithm

The solution algorithm requires a linear nested IF statement to calculate the sales tax.

```
Process_customer_record
    Read cust_name, purch_amt, tax_code
    IF tax_code = 0 THEN
        sales_tax = 0
    ELSE
        IF tax_code = 1 THEN
            sales_tax = purch_amt * 0.03
        ELSE
            IF tax_code = 2 THEN
                sales_tax = purch_amt * 0.05
            ELSE
                sales_tax = purch_amt * 0.07
            ENDIF
        ENDIF
    ENDIF
    total_amt = purch_amt + sales_tax
    Print cust_name, purch_amt, sales_tax, total_amt
END
```

C   Desk checking

Two sets of valid input data for purchase amount and tax code will be used
to check the algorithm.

(i) Input data:

	First data set	Second data set
purch_amt	10.00	20.00
tax_code	0	2

(ii) Expected results:

	First data set	Second data set
sales_tax	0	1.00
total_amt	10.00	21.00

Note that when desk checking the logic, the whole linear nested IF
statement (13 lines of pseudocode) is counted as a single pseudocode
statement.

(iii) Desk check table:

Statement	purch_amt	tax_code	sales_tax	total_amt	IFstatement executed?
First Pass					
Read	10.00	0			
IF			0		IF tax_code = 0
total_amt				10.00	
Print	yes		yes	yes	
Second Pass					
Read	20.00	2			
IF			1.00		IF tax_code = 2
total_amt				21.00	
Print	yes		yes	yes	

As the expected result for the two test cases matches the calculated result,
the algorithm is correct.

EXAMPLE 4.3   *Calculate employee's pay*

A program is required by a company to read an employee's number, pay rate
and the number of hours worked in a week. The program is then to compute
the employee's weekly pay and print it along with the input data.

According to the company's rules, no employee may be paid for more than 60 hours per week, and the maximum hourly rate is $25.00 per hour. If more than 35 hours are worked, then payment for the overtime hours worked is calculated at time-and-a-half. If the hours worked field or the hourly rate field is out of range, then the input data and an appropriate message is to be <u>printed</u> and the employee's weekly pay is not to be calculated.

A Defining diagram

Input	Processing	Output
emp_no	Read employee details	emp_no
pay_rate	Validate input fields	pay_rate
hrs_worked	Calculate employee pay	hrs_worked
	Print employee details	emp_weekly_pay
		error_message

B Solution algorithm

The solution to this problem will require a series of simple IF and nested IF statements. Firstly, the variables 'pay_rate' and 'hrs_worked' must be validated, and if either is found to be out of range then an appropriate message is to be placed into a variable called 'error_message'.

The employee's weekly pay is only to be calculated if the input variables 'pay_rate' and 'hrs_worked' are valid, so another variable, 'valid_input_fields', will be used to indicate to the program whether or not these input fields are valid.

Boolean variables

The variable valid_input_fields is a Boolean variable; that is, it may contain only one of two possible values (true or false). When using the IF statement with a Boolean variable, the IF statement can be simplified in pseudocode, as follows:

```
IF valid_input_fields = true THEN
    statement
ENDIF
```

can be simplified to imply '= true', and so can be written as:

```
IF valid_input_fields THEN
    statement
ENDIF
```

Similarly, if we want to test if valid_input_fields is false, we can say in pseudocode:

```
IF NOT valid_input_fields THEN
    statement
ENDIF
```

The variable valid_input_fields acts as an internal switch or flag to the program. It will initially be set to true, and will be assigned the value false if one of the input fields is found to be invalid. The employee's weekly pay will be calculated only if valid_input_fields is true.

```
Compute_employee_pay
      Set valid_input_fields to true
      Set error_message to blank
      Read emp_no, pay_rate, hrs_worked
      IF pay_rate > $25 THEN
            error_message = 'Pay rate exceeds $25.00'
            valid_input_fields = false
            Print emp_no, pay_rate, hrs_worked, error_message
      ENDIF
      IF hrs_worked > 60 THEN
            error_message = 'Hours worked exceeds limit of 60'
            valid_input_fields = false
            Print emp_no, pay_rate, hrs_worked, error_message
      ENDIF
      IF valid_input_fields THEN
            IF hrs_worked ≤ 35 THEN
                  emp_weekly_pay = pay_rate * hrs_worked
            ELSE
                  overtime_hrs = hrs_worked − 35
                  overtime_pay = overtime_hrs * pay_rate * 1.5
                  emp_weekly_pay = (pay_rate * 35) + overtime_pay
            ENDIF
            Print emp_no, pay_rate, hrs_worked, emp_weekly_pay
      ENDIF
END
```

In this solution there are two separate functions to be performed in the algorithm: the validation of the input data, and the calculation and printing of the employee's weekly pay. These two tasks could have been separated into modules before the algorithm was developed in pseudocode (see Chapter 7).

C   Desk checking

Two sets of valid input data for pay rate and hours worked will be used to check this algorithm.

(i)   Input data:

	First data set	Second data set
pay_rate	10.00	40.00
hrs_worked	40	35

(ii) Expected results:

	First data set	Second data set
pay_rate	10.00	40.00
hrs_worked	40	35
emp_weekly_pay	425.00	–
error_message	blank	Pay rate exceeds $25.00

(iii) Desk check table:

statement	pay rate	hrs worked	overtime hrs	overtime pay	emp weekly pay	valid input fields	error message	IF statement executed?
First Pass								
Initialise						true		
Initialise							blank	
Read	10.00	40						
IF								no
IF								no
IF			5	75.00	425.00			valid input fields
Print	yes	yes				yes		
Second Pass								
Initialise						true		
Initialise							blank	
Read	40.00	35						
IF						false	Pay rate exceeds $25.00	Pay rate >25.00
Print	yes	yes					yes	
IF								no
IF								no

4.3   THE CASE STRUCTURE

The case control structure in pseudocode is another way of expressing a linear nested IF statement. It is used in pseudocode for two reasons: it can be directly translated into many high-level languages, and it makes the pseudocode easier to write and understand. Nested IFs often look cumbersome in pseudocode and depend on correct structure and indentation for readability. Let us look at the example used earlier in this chapter:

```
IF record_code = 'A' THEN
    increment counter_A
ELSE
    IF record_code = 'B' THEN
        increment counter_B
    ELSE
        IF record_code = 'C' THEN
            increment counter_C
        ELSE
            increment error_counter
        ENDIF
    ENDIF
ENDIF
```

This linear nested IF structure can be replaced with a case control structure. Case is not really an additional control structure. It simplifies the basic selection control structure and extends it from a choice between two values to a choice from multiple values. In one case structure, several alternative logical paths can be represented. In pseudocode, the keywords CASE OF and ENDCASE serve to identify the structure, with the multiple values indented, as follows:

```
CASE OF single variable
    value_1 : statement block_1
    value_2 : statement block_2
            ⋮
    value_n : statement block_n
    value_other : statement block_other
ENDCASE
```

The path followed in the case structure depends on the value of the variable specified in the CASE OF clause. If the variable contains value_1 then statement block_1 is executed; if it contains value_2, then statement block_2 is executed, and so on. The value other is included in the event that the variable contains none of the listed values. We can now rewrite the above linear nested IF statement with a case statement, as follows:

```
CASE OF record_code
    'A'     : increment counter_A
    'B'     : increment counter_B
    'C'     : increment counter_C
    other  : increment error_counter
ENDCASE
```

In both forms of pseudocode the processing logic is exactly the same. However, the case solution is much more readable.

Let us now look again at Example 4.2. The solution algorithm for this example was earlier expressed as a linear nested IF statement, but it could equally have been expressed as a CASE statement.

EXAMPLE 4.4   *Process customer record*

A program is required to <u>read</u> a customer's name, a purchase amount and a tax code. The tax code has been validated and will be one of the following:

0   tax exempt (0%)
1   state sales tax only (3%)
2   federal and state sales tax (5%)
3   special sales tax (7%)

The program must then <u>compute</u> the sales tax and the total amount due and <u>print</u> the customer's name, purchase amount, sales tax and total amount due.

A   Defining diagram

Input	Processing	Output
cust_name	Read customer details	cust_name
purch_amt	Compute sales tax	purch_amt
tax_code	Compute total amount	sales_tax
	Print customer details	total_amt

B   Solution algorithm

The solution algorithm will be expressed using a CASE statement.

```
Process_customer_record
    Read cust_name, purch_amt, tax_code
    CASE OF tax_code
        0 : sales_tax = 0
        1 : sales_tax = purch_amt * 0.03
        2 : sales_tax = purch_amt * 0.05
        3 : sales_tax = purch_amt * 0.07
    ENDCASE
    total_amt = purch_amt + sales_tax
    Print cust_name, purch_amt, sales_tax, total_amt
END
```

C   Desk checking

Two sets of valid input data for purchase amount and tax code will be used to check the algorithm. Note that the case structure serves as a single pseudocode statement.

(i) Input data:

	First data set	Second data set
purch_amt	10.00	20.00
tax_code	0	2

(ii) Expected results:

	First data set	Second data set
sales_tax	0	1.00
total_amt	10.00	21.00

(iii) Desk check table:

Statement	purch_amt	tax_code	sales_tax	total_amt	CASE statement executed?
First Pass					
Read	10.00	0			
CASE			0		CASE 0
total_amt				10.00	
Print	yes		yes	yes	
Second Pass					
Read	20.00	2			
CASE			1.00		CASE 2
total_amt				21.00	
Print	yes		yes	yes	

As the expected result matches the actual result the algorithm is shown to be correct.

4.4 CHAPTER SUMMARY

This chapter covered the selection control structure in detail. Descriptions and pseudocode examples were given for simple selection, null ELSE, combined IF and nested IF statements. Several solution algorithms which used the selection structure were developed.

The case structure was introduced as a means of expressing a linear nested IF statement in a simpler and more concise form. Case is available in many high-level languages, and so is a useful construct to write in pseudocode.

PROGRAMMING PROBLEMS

Construct a solution algorithm for the following programming problems. Your solution should contain: a defining diagram, a pseudocode algorithm, and a desk check of the algorithm.

1   Design an algorithm which will prompt a terminal operator for the price of an article and a pricing code. Your program is then to calculate a discount rate according to the pricing code and print to the screen the original price of the article, the discount amount and the new discounted price. The pricing code and accompanying discount amount are to be calculated as follows:

Pricing code	Discount rate
H	50%
F	40%
T	33%
Q	25%
Z	0%

If the pricing code is Z, then the words 'No discount' are to be printed on the screen. If the pricing code is not H, Q, T, F or Z, then the words 'Invalid pricing code' are to be printed.

2   Design an algorithm which will prompt an operator for a student's serial number and the student's exam score out of 100. Your program is then to match the exam score to a letter grade and print the grade to the screen. The letter grade is to be calculated as follows:

Exam Score	Assigned Grade
90 and above	A
80 – 89	B
70 – 79	C
60 – 69	D
below 60	F

3   Design a program which will read two numbers and an integer code from the screen. The value of the code should be 1, 2, 3 or 4. If the value of the code is 1 then compute the sum of the two numbers. If the code is 2 compute the difference (first minus second). If the code is 3, compute the product of the two numbers. If the code is 4 and the second number is not zero, then compute the quotient (first number divided by second). The program is then to print the two numbers, the integer code and the computed result to the screen.

4   A transaction record on a Sales Commission File contains the retail price of an item sold, a transaction code which indicates the sales commission category to which an item can belong, and the employee number of the person who sold the item. The transaction code can contain the values S, M or L which indicate that the percentage commission will be 5%, 7% or 10% respectively. Construct an algorithm which will read a record on the file, calculate the commission owing for that record, and print the retail price, commission and employee number.

5   A glass return company requires a program which will calculate the amount of credit due to a customer who returns cases of empty bottles. (One case contains 10 bottles.) Input to the program is a record containing the customer's name and a number. This number contains the number of full or partly full cases of empty bottles the customer has returned (e.g. 8.5 indicates 8 full cases and one half-full case). If a case returned by a customer is more than half full, it is to be counted as full. If 8 or more cases are returned, the customer is to receive $4.00 per case, otherwise the customer receives $3.50 per case. The program is to print the customer's name, the number of cases returned, the number of full cases credited and the credit amount due.

6   A home mortgage authority requires a deposit on a home loan according to the following schedule:

Loan $	Deposit
less than 25,000	5% of loan value
25,000 – 49,000	$1250 + 10% of loan over $25,000
50,000 – 100,000	$5000 + 25% of loan over $50,000

Loans in excess of $100,000 are not allowed. Design a program which will read a loan amount and compute and print the required deposit.

Repetition control structures

DESK CHECKING

DOWHILE
you've got
nothing better
to do ...

5.1 REPETITION USING THE DOWHILE STRUCTURE

The solution algorithms developed so far have one characteristic in common: they show the program logic required to process just one set of input values. However, most programs require the same logic to be repeated for several sets of data. The most efficient way to deal with this situation is to establish a looping structure in the algorithm that will cause the processing logic to be repeated a number of times.

In Chapter 2, the DOWHILE construct was introduced as the pseudocode representation of a repetitive loop. Its format is:

```
DOWHILE condition p is true
    statement block
ENDDO
```

As the DOWHILE loop is a leading decision loop, the following processing takes place:

(a) The logical condition p is tested.
(b) If condition p is found to be true, then the statements within the statement block are executed once. Control then returns to the retesting of condition p (step a).
(c) If condition p is found to be false, then control passes to the next statement after ENDDO and no further processing takes place within the loop.

As a result, the DOWHILE structure will continue to repeat a group of statements while a condition remains true. As soon as the condition becomes false, the construct is exited.

There are two important considerations about which you must be aware before designing a DOWHILE loop.

Firstly, the testing of the condition is at the beginning of the loop. This means that the programmer may need to perform some initial processing to adequately set up the condition before it can be tested.

Secondly, the only way to terminate the loop is to render the DOWHILE condition false. This means you must set up some process within the statement block which will eventually change the condition so that the condition becomes false. Failure to do this results in an endless loop.

EXAMPLE 5.1 *Fahrenheit–Celsius conversion*

Every day, a weather station receives 15 temperatures expressed in degrees Fahrenheit. A program is to be written which will <u>accept</u> each Fahrenheit temperature, <u>convert</u> it to Celsius and <u>display</u> the converted temperature to the screen. After 15 temperatures have been processed, the words 'All temperatures processed' are to be <u>displayed</u> on the screen.

A Defining diagram

Input	Processing	Output
f_temp (15 temperatures)	Get Fahrenheit temperatures Convert temperatures Display Celsius temperatures Display screen message	c_temp (15 temperatures)

The defining diagram still only lists what needs to be done; the equation to convert the temperature will not need to be known until the algorithm is developed.

Having defined the input, output and processing, you are ready to outline a solution to the problem. This can be done by writing down the control structures needed and any extra variables which are to be used in the solution algorithm. In this example you need:

- a DOWHILE structure to repeat the necessary processing, and
- a counter, initialised at zero, which will control the fifteen repetitions. This counter, called temperature_count, will contain the number of temperatures read and processed.

You should now write down the solution algorithm.

B Solution algorithm

```
Fahrenheit_Celsius_conversion
    Set temperature_count to zero
    DOWHILE temperature_count < 15
        Prompt operator for f_temp
        Get f_temp
        Compute c_temp = (f_temp − 32) * 5/9
        Display c_temp
        Add 1 to temperature_count
    ENDDO
    Display 'All temperatures processed' to the screen
END
```

Note that the temperature_count variable is initialised before the loop, tested in the DOWHILE condition at the top of the loop, and incremented within the body of the loop. It is essential that the variable which controls the loop is acted upon in these three places. Notice also that the statement which alters the value of temperature_count in the loop is the last statement in the statement block. That is, immediately after incrementing temperature_count, its value will be tested when control returns to the DOWHILE condition at the top of the loop.

This solution algorithm could also have been expressed using the keywords
WHILE...DO and ENDWHILE, as follows:

```
Fahrenheit_Celsius_conversion
    Set temperature_count to zero
    WHILE temperature_count < 15 DO
        Prompt operator for f_temp
        Get f_temp
        Compute c_temp = (f_temp – 32) * 5/9
        Display c_temp
        Add 1 to temperature_count
    ENDWHILE
    Display 'All temperatures processed' to the screen
END
```

This is identical to the first algorithm; only the repetition keywords used are
different.

C   Desk checking

Although the program will require 15 records to process properly, it is still
only necessary to check the algorithm at this stage with two valid sets of
data.

(i)   Input data:

	First data set	Second data set
f_temp	32	50

(ii) Expected results:

	First data set	Second data set
c_temp	0	10

(iii) Desk check table:

Statement	temperature_ count	DOWHILE condition	f_temp	c_temp
Initialise	0			
DOWHILE		true		
Get			32	
Compute				0
Display				yes
Add	1			
DOWHILE		true		
Get			50	
Compute				10
Display				yes
Add	2			

Desk checking this algorithm shows the exact processing of a DOWHILE loop. There is some initial processing (first statement) which will be executed only once. Then the DOWHILE condition is tested and found to be true. The body of the loop is then executed before returning to the testing of the DOWHILE condition. Processing will continue to repeat until the DOWHILE condition becomes false, i.e. until the temperature counter equals 15.

Although only two test cases were used to desk check the algorithm, you can see that, given more test cases, the temperature counter will eventually reach 15, and so the looping will cease.

Let us now look at a problem where an unknown number of records are to be processed. In this situation, you cannot use a counter to control the loop, so another method is required. Often this takes the form of a trailer record, or sentinel. This sentinel is a special record or value placed at the end of valid data to signify the end of that data. It must contain a value which is clearly distinguishable from the other data to be processed. It is referred to as a sentinel because it indicates that no more data follows.

EXAMPLE 5.2 *Print examination scores*

A program is required to read and print a series of names and exam scores for students enrolled in a mathematics course. The class average is to be computed and printed at the end of the report. Scores can range from 0 to 100. The last record contains a blank name and a score of 999 and is not to be included in the calculations.

A Defining diagram

Input	Processing	Output
name	Read student details	name
exam_score	Print student details	exam_score
	Compute average score	average_score
	Print average score	

You will need to consider the following requirements when establishing a solution algorithm:

- a DOWHILE structure to control the reading of exam scores, until it reaches a score of 999,
- an accumulator for total scores, namely total_score, and
- an accumulator for the total students, namely total_students.

B Solution algorithm

```
Print_examination_scores
    Set total_score to zero
    Set total_students to zero
    Read name, exam_score
    DOWHILE exam_score not = 999
        Add 1 to total_students
        Print name, exam_score
        Add exam_score to total_score
        Read name, exam_score
    ENDDO
    IF total_students not = zero THEN
        average_score = total_score / total_students
        Print average_score
    ENDIF
END
```

This solution algorithm is a typical example of the basic algorithm design required for processing sequential files of data. There is an unknown number of records, so the condition which controls the exam score processing is the testing for the trailer record (Record_999). It is this test which appears in the DOWHILE clause (DOWHILE exam_score not = 999).

However, this test cannot be made until at least one exam score has been read. Hence, the initial processing, which sets up the condition, is a Read statement immediately before the DOWHILE clause (Read name, exam_score). This is known as a priming Read, and its use is extremely important when processing sequential files.

The algorithm will require another Read statement, this time within the body of the loop. Its position is also important. The trailer record must not be included in the calculation of average score, so each time an exam score is read, it must be tested for a 999 value, before further processing can take place. For this reason, the Read statement is placed at the end of the loop, immediately before ENDDO, so that its value can be tested when control returns to the DOWHILE condition. As soon as the trailer record has been read, control will exit from the loop to the next statement after ENDDO, which is the calculation of average_score.

The priming Read before the DOWHILE condition, together with the subsequent Read within the loop, immediately before the ENDDO statement, form the basic framework for DOWHILE repetitions in pseudocode. In general, all algorithms using a DOWHILE construct to process a sequential file should have the same basic pattern, as follows:

```
Process_sequential_file
    Initial processing
    Read first record
    DOWHILE more records exist
        Process this record
        Read next record
    ENDDO
    Final processing
END
```

C   Desk checking

Two valid records and a trailer record should be sufficient to desk check this algorithm.

(i) Input data:

	First record	Second record	Third record
score	50	100	999

(ii) Expected results:

1st name, and score of 50
2nd name, and score of 100
Average score   75

(iii) Desk check table:

Statement	total_ score	total_ students	exam_ score	DOWHILE condition	average_ score
Initialise	0	0			
Read			50		
DOWHILE				true	
Add		1			
Print			yes		
Add	50				
Read			100		
DOWHILE				true	
Add		2			
Print			yes		
Add	150				
Read			999		
DOWHILE				false	
Compute					75
Print					yes

The expected results are confirmed, which proves that the algorithm is correct for this set of data.

EXAMPLE 5.3   *Process student enrolments*

A program is required which will <u>read</u> a file of student records, and <u>select</u> and <u>print</u> only those students enrolled in a course unit named Programming I. Each student record contains student number, name, address, postcode, gender and course unit number. The course unit number for Programming I is 18500. Three totals are to be <u>printed</u> at the end of the report: total females enrolled in the course, total males enrolled in the course, and total students enrolled in the course.

A Defining diagram

Input	Processing	Output
student_record	Read student records	selected student
• student_no	Select student records	records
• name	Print selected records	totals
• address	Compute total females enrolled	
• postcode	Compute total males enrolled	
• gender	Compute total students enrolled	
• course_unit	Print totals	

You will need to consider the following requirements, when establishing a solution algorithm:

- a DOWHILE structure to perform the repetition,
- an IF statement to select the required students, and
- accumulators for the three total fields.

Note that there is no trailer record for this student file. In cases like this, the terms 'more data', 'more records', 'records exist' or 'not EOF' (end of file) can be used in the DOWHILE or WHILE...DO condition clause. For example, these are all equivalent conditions:

```
DOWHILE more data
DOWHILE more records
DOWHILE records exist
DOWHILE NOT EOF
WHILE success DO
```

By expressing the condition in this way, you leave it to the computer to indicate to the program when there are no more records in the file. This occurs when an attempt is made to read a record but no more records exist. A signal is sent to the program to indicate that there are no more records, so the 'DOWHILE more records' or 'DOWHILE NOT EOF' clause is rendered false.

B Solution algorithm

```
Process_student_enrolments
      Set total_females_enrolled to zero
      Set total_males_enrolled to zero
      Set total_students_enrolled to zero
      Read student record
      DOWHILE records exist
          IF course_unit = 18500 THEN
              print student details
              increment total_students_enrolled
              IF student_gender = female THEN
                  increment total_females_enrolled
              ELSE
                  increment total_males_enrolled
              ENDIF
          ENDIF
          Read student record
      ENDDO
      Print total_females_enrolled
      Print total_males_enrolled
      Print total_students_enrolled
END
```

This solution algorithm uses the same basic framework as the previous example. A non-linear nested IF statement was used to determine the required selection logic.

C Desk checking

Three valid student records should be sufficient to desk check this algorithm. Since student_no, name, address, and postcode are not operated upon in this algorithm, they do not need to be given in the input data sets.

(i) Input data:

	First record	Second record	Third record
course_unit	20000	18500	18500
gender	F	F	M

(ii) Expected results:

Student number, name, address, postcode, F (2nd student)
Student number, name, address, postcode, M (3rd student)

Total females enrolled	1
Total males enrolled	1
Total students enrolled	2

(iii) Desk check table:

The non-linear nested IF statement in this example will be considered a single statement when desk checking the algorithm.

statement	course_ unit	gender	DOWHILE condition	IF condition	total_ females_ enrolled	total_ males_ enrolled	total_ students_ enrolled
Initialise					0	0	0
Read	20000	F					
DOWHILE			true				
IF				false			
Read	18500	F					
DOWHILE			true				
IF	Print	Print		true			1
IF				true	1		
Read	18500	M					
DOWHILE			true				
IF	Print	Print		true			2
IF				false		1	
Read	EOF						
DOWHILE			false				
Print					yes	yes	yes

5.2   REPETITION USING THE REPEAT...UNTIL STRUCTURE

The REPEAT...UNTIL structure is similar to the DOWHILE structure, in that a group of statements are repeated in accordance with a specified condition. However, where the DOWHILE structure tests the condition at the beginning of the loop, a REPEAT...UNTIL structure tests the condition at the end of the loop. This means that the statements within the loop will be executed once before the condition is tested. If the condition is false, the statements will then be repeated UNTIL the condition becomes true.

The format of the REPEAT...UNTIL structure is:

```
REPEAT
    statement
    statement
       :
UNTIL condition is true
```

You can see that REPEAT...UNTIL is a trailing decision loop; the statements are executed once before the condition is tested.

There are two other considerations about which you need to be aware before using REPEAT...UNTIL.

Firstly, REPEAT...UNTIL loops are executed when the condition is false; it is only when the condition becomes true that repetition ceases. Thus the logic of the condition clause of the REPEAT...UNTIL structure is the opposite of DOWHILE. For instance, 'DOWHILE more records' is equivalent to 'REPEAT...UNTIL no more records', and 'DOWHILE number NOT = 99' is equivalent to 'REPEAT...UNTIL number = 99'.

Secondly, the statements within a REPEAT...UNTIL structure will always be executed at least once. As a result, there is no need for a priming Read when using REPEAT...UNTIL. One Read statement at the beginning of the loop is sufficient.

Let us now compare an algorithm which uses a DOWHILE structure with the same problem using a REPEAT...UNTIL structure. Consider the following DOWHILE loop:

```
Process_student_records
    Set student_count to zero
    Read student record
    DOWHILE student number NOT = 999
        Write student record
        Increment student_count
        Read student record
    ENDDO
    Print student_count
END
```

This can be rewritten (incorrectly) as a trailing decision loop, using the REPEAT...UNTIL structure as follows:

```
Process_student_records
    Set student_count to zero
    REPEAT
        Read student record          INCORRECT
        Write student record         REPEAT...UNTIL logic
        Increment student_count
    UNTIL student number = 999
    Print student_count
END
```

This algorithm is incorrect, because the statements within the loop will be repeated just one time too many. Instead of immediately terminating the repetition once the trailer record has been read (Read student record), there are two more statements in the loop which will be executed, before the condition is tested. That is, the trailer record will be written to the file and added to student_count before establishing that it is the trailer record. To avoid this, logic must be included which will prevent data being processed once the trailer record has been read. This logic takes the form of an IF statement immediately after the Read statement, as follows:

```
Process_student_records
    Set student_count to zero
    REPEAT
        Read student record
        IF student number NOT = 999 THEN          CORRECT
            Write student record                  REPEAT...UNTIL logic
            Increment student_count
        ENDIF
    UNTIL student number = 999
    Print student_count
END
```

REPEAT...UNTIL loops are used less frequently in pseudocode than DOWHILE loops for sequential file processing because of this extra IF statement required within the loop.

The majority of examples given in this book will use the DOWHILE construct in preference to REPEAT...UNTIL because of its simple structure. However, the following programming example does use REPEAT...UNTIL.

EXAMPLE 5.4 *Process inventory items*

A program is required to <u>read</u> a series of inventory records which contain item number, item description and stock figure. The last record in the file has an item number of zero. The program is to <u>produce</u> a 'Low Stock Items' report, by <u>printing</u> only those records which have a stock figure of less than 20 items. A heading is to be <u>printed</u> at the top of the report and a total low stock item count to be <u>printed</u> at the end.

A Defining diagram

Input	Processing	Output
inventory record	Read inventory records	heading
• item_number	Select low stock items	selected records
• item_description	Print low stock records	• item_number
• stock_figure	Print total low stock records	• item_description
		• stock_figure
		total_low_stock_items

You will need to consider the following requirements when establishing a solution algorithm:

- a REPEAT...UNTIL to perform the repetition (a DOWHILE could also have been used),
- an IF statement to select stock figures of less than 20,
- an accumulator for total_low_stock_items, and
- an extra IF, within the REPEAT loop, to ensure the trailer record is not processed.

B1 Solution algorithm using REPEAT...UNTIL

```
Process_inventory_records
      Set total_low_stock_items to zero
      Print 'Low Stock Items' heading
      REPEAT
            Read inventory record
            IF item_number > zero THEN
                  IF stock_figure < 20 THEN
                        print item_number, item_description, stock_figure
                        increment total_low_stock_items
                  ENDIF
            ENDIF
      UNTIL item_number = zero
      Print total_low_stock_items
END
```

The solution algorithm has a simple structure, with a single Read statement at the beginning of the REPEAT...UNTIL loop and an extra IF statement within the loop to ensure the trailer record is not incorrectly incremented into the total_low_stock_items accumulator.

B2 Solution algorithm using DOWHILE

```
Process_inventory_records
      Set total_low_stock_items to zero
      Print 'Low Stock Items' heading
      Read inventory record
      DOWHILE item_number > zero
            IF stock_figure < 20 THEN
                  print item_number, item_description, stock_figure
                  increment total_low_stock_items
            ENDIF
            Read inventory record
      ENDDO
      Print total_low_stock_items
END
```

This solution, using DOWHILE, also has simple structure, with a priming Read and a Read at the end of the loop just before ENDDO. When a record containing an item number of zero is read, the DOWHILE condition will become false and the looping will cease.

C Desk checking

The first solution algorithm, which uses a REPEAT...UNTIL structure, will be the algorithm which is desk checked. Two valid records and a trailer record (item number equal to zero) will be used to test the algorithm:

(i) Input data:

	First record	Second record	Trailer record
item_number	123	124	0
stock_figure	8	25	

(ii) Expected results:

Low Stock Items
123   8   (first record)

Total Low Stock Items = 1

(iii) Desk check table:

Statement	item_ number	stock_ figure	REPEAT UNTIL	first IF condition	second IF condition	total_low stock_items	heading
Initialise						0	
Print							yes
Read	123	8					
IF				true			
IF	Print	Print			true	1	
UNTIL			false				
Read	124	25					
IF				true			
IF					false		
UNTIL			false				
Read	0						
IF				false			
UNTIL			true				
Print						yes	

5.3 COUNTED REPETITION CONSTRUCTS

Counted repetition occurs when the exact number of loop iterations is known in advance. The execution of the loop is controlled by a loop index, and instead of using DOWHILE, or REPEAT...UNTIL, the simple keyword DO is used as follows:

```
DO loop_index = initial_value to final_value
    statement block
ENDDO
```

The DO loop does more than just repeat the statement block. It will:

1   initialise the loop_index to the required initial_value,
2   increment the loop_index by 1 for each pass through the loop,
3   test the value of loop_index at the beginning of each loop to ensure that it is within the stated range of values, and
4   terminate the loop when the loop_index has exceeded the specified final_value.

In other words, a counted repetition construct will perform the initialising, incrementing and testing of the loop counter automatically. It will also terminate the loop once the required number of repetitions have been executed.

Let us look again at Example 5.1, which processes 15 temperatures at a weather station each day. The solution algorithm can be redesigned to use a DO loop.

EXAMPLE 5.5   *Fahrenheit–Celsius conversion*

Every day, a weather station receives 15 temperatures expressed in degrees Fahrenheit. A program is to be written which will <u>accept</u> each Fahrenheit temperature, <u>convert</u> it to Celsius and <u>display</u> the converted temperature to the screen. After 15 temperatures have been processed, the words 'All temperatures processed' are to be <u>displayed</u> on the screen.

A   *Defining diagram*

Input	Processing	Output
f_temp	Get Fahrenheit temperatures	c_temp
(15 temperatures)	Convert temperatures	(15 temperatures)
	Display Celsius temperatures	
	Display screen message	

B Solution algorithm

The solution will require a DO loop and a loop counter (temperature_count) to process the repetition.

```
Fahrenheit_Celsius_conversion
    DO temperature_count = 1 to 15
        Prompt operator for f_temp
        Get f_temp
        Compute c_temp = (f_temp - 32) * 5/9
        Display c_temp
    ENDDO
    Display 'All temperatures processed' to the screen
END
```

Note that the DO loop controls all the repetition:

- it initialises temperature_count to 1,
- it increments temperature_count by 1 for each pass through the loop,
- it tests temperature_count at the beginning of each pass to ensure that it is within the range 1 to 15, and
- it automatically terminates the loop once temperature_count has exceeded 15.

C Desk checking

Two valid records should be sufficient to test the algorithm for correctness. It is not necessary to check the DO loop construct for all 15 records.

(i) Input data:

	First data set	Second data set
f_temp	32	50

(ii) Expected results:

	First data set	Second data set
c_temp	0	10

(iii) Desk check table:

Statement	temperature_count	DO	f_temp	c_temp
DO	1	set to 1		
Get			32	
Compute				0
Display				yes
DO	2	increment		
Get			50	
Compute				10
Display				yes

Desk checking the algorithm with the two input test cases indicates that the expected results have been achieved.

A requirement of counted repetition loops is that the exact number of input data items or records needs to be known before the algorithm can be written. This is an artificial situation in real life, but counted repetition loops are used extensively with arrays or tables.

Arrays

An array is a data structure which is made up of a number of variables which all have the same data type; for example, all the exam scores for a class. By using an array, you can associate a single variable name, such as 'scores', with the entire collection of data. The individual elements of the array can then be accessed by the use of an index or subscript beside the name of the array, for example 'scores(3)'. The index indicates the position of an element within an array; for example scores(3) points to the third element of the array scores.

You may often need to process the elements of an array in sequence, starting with the first element. This can be accomplished easily in pseudocode with a DO loop, as in the next example.

EXAMPLE 5.6   *Process exam scores*

Design a program which will <u>prompt</u> for and <u>receive</u> 18 examination scores from a mathematics test, <u>compute</u> the class average, and <u>display</u> all the scores and the class average to the screen.

A Defining diagram

Input	Processing	Output
scores	Prompt for scores	scores
	Get exam scores	average_score
	Compute average_score	
	Display scores	
	Display average_score	

B Solution algorithm

This is an example of a counted repetition loop as we know that there are exactly 18 exam scores. You will need to consider the following requirements:

- an array to store the exam scores, i.e. 'scores',
- an index to identify each element in the array,
- one DO loop to accept the scores, and
- another DO loop to display the scores to the screen.

```
Process_exam_scores
    Set total_score to zero
    DO index = 1 to 18
        Prompt operator for score
        Get scores(index)
        total_score = total_score + scores(index)
    ENDDO
    compute average_score = total_score / 18
    DO index = 1 to 18
        Display scores(index)
    ENDDO
    Display average_score
END
```

(c) Desk checking

(i) Input data:

Input data set
18 scores of 100

scores

(ii) Expected results:

Input data set
100

average_score

(iii) Desk check table:

Statement	total_ score	first DO loop	second DO loop	average_ score	scores
Initialise	0				
DO	1800	OK			100 × 18
Compute				100	
DO			OK		displayed
Display				yes	

5.4   CHAPTER SUMMARY

This chapter covered the repetition control structure in detail. Descriptions and pseudocode examples were given for DOWHILE, REPEAT...UNTIL, and counted repetition loops. Arrays were introduced and an example which used a counted repetition loop on an array was developed. Several solution algorithms which used each of the three control structures were defined, developed and desk checked.

We saw that most of the solution algorithms had the same general pattern. This pattern consisted of:

1   some initial processing before the loop;
2   some processing for each record within the loop; and
3   some final processing once the loop has been exited.

Expressed as a solution algorithm using the DOWHILE construct this basic pattern was developed as a general solution:

```
Process_sequential_file
    Initial processing
    Read first record
    DOWHILE more records exist
        Process this record
        Read next record
    ENDDO
    Final processing
END
```

5.5   PROGRAMMING PROBLEMS

Construct a solution algorithm for the following programming problems. Your solution should contain:

- a defining diagram,
- a pseudocode algorithm, and
- a desk check of the algorithm.

1   Design an algorithm which will prompt for, receive, and total a collection of payroll amounts entered at the terminal until a sentinel amount of −99 is entered. After the sentinel has been entered, display the total payroll amount on the screen.

2   Design an algorithm which will read a series of integers at the terminal. The first integer is special, as it will indicate how many more integers will follow. Your algorithm is to compute and print the sum and average of the integers, excluding the first integer, and display these values to the screen.

3   Design an algorithm which will process the weekly employee time cards for all the employees of an organisation. Each employee time card will have three data items: an employee number, an hourly wage rate, and the number of hours worked during a given week. Each employee is to be paid time-and-a-half for all hours worked over 35. A tax amount of 15% of gross salary will be deducted. The output to the screen should display the employee's number and net pay. At the end of the run, display the total payroll amount and the average net amount paid.

4   Design a program which will read a file of employee records containing employee number, employee name, hourly pay rate, regular hours worked and overtime hours worked. The company pays its employees weekly, according to the following rules:

> regular pay = regular hours * hourly rate of pay
> overtime pay = overtime hours * hourly rate of pay * 1.5
> total pay = regular pay + overtime pay

Your program is to read the input data on each employee's record and compute and print the employee's total pay, on the 'Weekly Payroll Report'. All input data and calculated amounts are to appear on the report. A total payroll amount is to appear at the end of the report.

5   Design a program which will read a file of product records, each containing the item number, item name, the quantity sold this year and the quantity sold last year. The program is to produce a 'Product List' showing the item number, item name, and the increase or decrease in the quantity sold for each item.

6   The first record of a set of records contains a bank account number and an opening balance. Each of the remaining records in the set contains the amount of a cheque drawn on that bank account. The trailer record contains a zero amount. Design a program which will read and print the account number and opening balance on a 'Statement of Account' report. The rest of the amounts are to be read and printed on the report, each with a new running balance. A closing balance is to be printed at the end of the report.

Pseudocode algorithms using sequence, selection and repetition

what a
complicated
chapter

Yeah!
I thought
this book was
supposed to be
SIMPLE!

6.1 EIGHT SOLUTION ALGORITHMS

This chapter develops solution algorithms to eight programming problems of increasing complexity. All the algorithms will use a combination of sequence, selection and repetition constructs. The algorithms have been designed to be interactive, to process sequential files or to process arrays. Reading these algorithms should consolidate the groundwork developed in the previous chapters.

Each programming problem will be defined, the control structures required will be determined, and a solution algorithm will be devised.

(a) Defining the problem

It is extremely important that you divide the problem into its three components: input, output and processing. The processing component should list the tasks to be performed, i.e. what needs to be done, not how. The verbs in each problem have been underlined to help identify the actions to be performed.

(b) The control structures required

Once the problem has been defined, write down the control structures (sequence, selection and repetition) which may be needed, as well as any extra variables which the solution may require.

(c) The solution algorithm

Having defined the problem and determined the required control structures, devise a solution algorithm and represent it using pseudocode. Each solution algorithm presented in this chapter is only one solution to the particular problem: many different solutions could be equally correct.

(d) Desk checking

You will need to desk check each of the algorithms with two or more test cases.

EXAMPLE 6.1 *Process number pairs*

Design an algorithm which will <u>prompt</u> for and <u>receive</u> pairs of numbers from an operator at a terminal and <u>display</u> their sum, product and average on the screen. If the calculated sum is over 200 then an asterisk is to be <u>displayed</u> beside the sum. The program is to terminate when a pair of zero values is entered.

A Defining diagram

Input	Processing	Output
number_1	Prompt for numbers	sum
number_2	Get two numbers	product
	Calculate sum	average
	Calculate product	'*'
	Calculate average	
	Display sum, product, average	
	Display '*'	

B Control structures required

1 A DOWHILE loop to control the repetition, and
2 An IF statement to determine if an asterisk is to be displayed.
3 Note the use of the NOT operand with the AND logical operator.

C Solution algorithm

```
Process_number_pairs
    Set sum to zero
    Prompt for number_1, number_2
    Get number_1, number_2
    DOWHILE NOT (number_1 = 0 AND number_2 = 0)
        sum = number_1 + number_2
        product = number_1 * number_2
        average = sum / 2
        IF sum > 200 THEN
            Display sum, '*', product, average,
        ELSE
            Display sum, product, average
        ENDIF
        Prompt for number_1, number_2
        Get number_1, number_2
    ENDDO
END
```

EXAMPLE 6.2 Print student records

A file of student records consists of 'S' records and 'U' records. An 'S' record contains the student's number, name, age, gender, address and attendance pattern; full time (F/T) or part time (P/T). A 'U' record contains the number and name of the unit or units in which the student has enrolled. There may be more than one 'U' record for each 'S' record. Design a solution algorithm which will <u>read</u> the file of student records and <u>print</u> only the student's number, name and address on a 'STUDENT LIST'.

A   Defining diagram

Input	Processing	Output
's' records	Print heading line	heading line
• number	Read student records	selected student records
• name	Select 's' records	• number
• address	Print selected records	• name
• age		• address
• gender		
• attendance_pattern		
'u' records		

B   Control structures required

1   A DOWHILE loop to control the repetition, and
2   An IF statement to select 'S' records.

C   Solution algorithm

```
Print_student_records
     Print 'STUDENT LIST' heading
     Read student record
     DOWHILE more records exist
          IF student record = 'S' record THEN
               print student_number, name, and address
          ENDIF
          Read student record
     ENDDO
END
```

EXAMPLE 6.3   *Print selected students*

Design a solution algorithm which will <u>read</u> the same student file as in Example 6.2, and <u>produce</u> a report of all female students who are enrolled part time. The report is to be headed 'PART TIME FEMALE STUDENTS' and is to <u>show</u> the student's number, name, address and age.

A Defining diagram

Input	Processing	Output
's' records	Print heading	heading line
• number	Read student records	selected student records
• name	Select P/T female students	• number
• address	Print selected records	• name
• age		• address
• gender		• age
• attendance_pattern		
'u' records		

B Control structures required

1 A DOWHILE loop to control the repetition, and
2 An IF statement or statements to select 'S', female and part-time (P/T) students.

C Solution algorithm

Several algorithms for this problem will be presented, and all are equally correct. The only place the algorithms differ is in the expression of the IF statement. It is interesting to compare the three different solutions.

Solution 1 uses a non-linear nested IF:

```
Produce_part_time_female_list
    Print 'PART TIME FEMALE STUDENTS' heading
    Read student record
    DOWHILE more records
        IF student record = 'S' record THEN
            IF attendance_pattern = P/T THEN
                IF gender = female THEN
                    Print student_number, name, address, age
                ENDIF
            ENDIF
        ENDIF
        Read student record
    ENDDO
END
```

Solution 2 uses a nested and compound IF statement:

```
Produce_part_time_female_list
     Print 'PART TIME FEMALE STUDENTS' heading
     Read student record
     DOWHILE more records
         IF student record = 'S' record THEN
             IF (attendance_pattern = P/T
             AND gender = female) THEN
                 Print student_number, name, address, age
             ENDIF
         ENDIF
         Read student record
     ENDDO
END
```

Solution 3 also uses a compound IF statement:

```
Produce_part_time_female_list
     Print 'PART TIME FEMALE STUDENTS' heading
     Read student record
     DOWHILE more records
         IF student record = 'S' record
         AND attendance_pattern = P/T
         AND gender = female THEN
             Print student_number, name, address, age
         ENDIF
         Read student record
     ENDDO
END
```

EXAMPLE 6.4   *Print and total selected students*

Design a solution algorithm which will <u>read</u> the same student file as in Example 6.3 and <u>produce</u> the same 'PART TIME FEMALE STUDENTS' report. In addition, you are to <u>print</u> at the end of the report the number of students who have been selected and listed, and the total number of students on the file.

A *Defining diagram*

Input	Processing	Output
's' records	Print heading	heading line
• number	Read student records	selected student records
• name	Select P/T female students	• number
• address	Print selected records	• name
• age	Compute total students	• address
• gender	Compute total selected students	• age
• attendance_pattern	Print totals	total_students
'u' records		total_selected_students

B *Control structures required*

1 A DOWHILE loop to control the repetition,

2 IF statements to select 'S', female and P/T students, and

3 Accumulators for total_selected_students and total_students.

C *Solution algorithm*

```
Produce_part_time_female_list
      Print 'PART TIME FEMALE STUDENTS' heading
      Set total_students to zero
      Set total_selected_students to zero
      Read student record
      DOWHILE records exist
          IF student record = 'S' record THEN
              increment total_students
              IF (attendance_pattern = P/T
              AND gender = female) THEN
                  increment total_selected_students
                  Print student_number, name, address, age
              ENDIF
          ENDIF
          Read student record
      ENDDO
      Print total_students
      Print total_selected_students
  END
```

Note the positions where the total accumulators are incremented. If these statements are not placed accurately within their respective IF statements, then the algorithm could produce erroneous results.

EXAMPLE 6.5 *Process integer array*

Design an algorithm which will <u>read</u> an array of 100 integer values and <u>count</u> the number of integers in the array which are greater than the average value of all the integers in the array. The algorithm is to <u>display</u> the average integer value and the count of integers greater than the average.

A Defining diagram

Input	Processing	Output
100 integer values	Read integer values	average
	Calculate average value	integer_count
	Compute count of selected integers	
	Display average value	
	Display selected integer count	

B Control structures required

1 an array of integer values, i.e. numbers
2 a DO loop to calculate the average of the integers, and
3 a DO loop to count the number of integers greater than the average.

C Solution algorithm

```
Process_integer_array
    Set integer_total to zero
    Set integer_count to zero
    DO index = 1 to 100
        integer_total = integer_total + numbers(index)
    ENDDO
    average = integer_total / 100
    DO index = 1 to 100
        IF numbers(index) > average THEN
            add 1 to integer_count
        ENDIF
    ENDDO
    Display average, integer_count
END
```

EXAMPLE 6.6 *Produce sales report*

Design a program which will <u>read</u> a file of sales records and <u>produce</u> a sales report. Each record in the file contains a customer's number, name, a sales amount and a tax code. The tax code is to be applied to the sales amount to determine the sales tax due for that sale, as follows:

tax code	sales tax
0	tax exempt
1	3%
2	5%

The report is to <u>print</u> a heading 'SALES REPORT', and detail lines listing the customer number, name, sales amount, sales tax and the total amount due from the customer.

A Defining diagram

Input	Processing	Output
sales records	Print heading	heading line
• customer_number	Read sales records	detail lines
• name	Calculate sales tax	• customer_number
• sales_amt	Calculate total amount	• name
• tax_code	Print customer details	• sales_amt
		• sales_tax
		• total_amt

B Control structures required

1   A WHILE...DO loop, to control the repetition, and
2   A case statement to calculate the sales_tax.

Assume that the tax_code field has been validated and will contain only a value of 0, 1 or 2.

C Solution algorithm

```
Produce_sales_report
    Print 'SALES REPORT' heading
    Read sales record
    WHILE success DO
        CASE of tax_code
            0 : sales_tax = 0
            1 : sales_tax = sales_amt * 0.03
            2 : sales_tax = sales_amt * 0.05
        ENDCASE
        total_amt = sales_amt + sales_tax
        Print customer_number, name, sales_amt, sales_tax, total_amt
        Read sales record
    ENDWHILE
END
```

A linear nested IF statement could have been used in place of the case statement in this example. The case statement, however, expresses the logic so simply that it should be used wherever appropriate.

EXAMPLE 6.7 *Student test results*

Design a solution algorithm which will <u>read</u> a file of student test results and <u>produce</u> a Student Test Grades report. Each test record contains the student number, name and test score (out of 50). The program is to <u>calculate</u> for each student the test score as a percentage and to <u>print</u> the student's number, name, test score (out of 50) and letter grade on the report. The letter grade is determined as follows:

A = 90 – 100%
B = 80 – 89%
C = 70 – 79%
D = 60 – 69%
F = 0 – 59%

A *Defining diagram*

Input	Processing	Output
student test records	Print heading	heading line
• student_number	Read student records	student details
• name	Calculate test percentage	• student_number
• test_score	Calculate letter grade	• name
	Print student details	• test_score
		• grade

B *Control structures required*

1   A DOWHILE loop to control the repetition,
2   A linear nested IF statement to calculate the grade, and
3   A formula to calculate the percentage.
    (The case construct cannot be used here, as it is not designed to cater for a range of values, e.g. 0 – 59%).

C   Solution algorithm

```
Print_student_results
    Print 'STUDENT TEST GRADES' heading
    Read student record
    DOWHILE not EOF
        percentage = test_score * 2
        IF percentage > 89 THEN
            grade = A
        ELSE
            IF percentage > 79 THEN
                grade = B
            ELSE
                IF percentage > 69 THEN
                    grade = C
                ELSE
                    IF percentage > 59 THEN
                        grade = D
                    ELSE
                        grade - F
                    ENDIF
                ENDIF
            ENDIF
        ENDIF
        Print student_number, name, test_score, grade
        Read student record
    ENDDO
END
```

Note that the linear nested IF has been worded so that all alternatives have been considered.

EXAMPLE 6.8   *Gas supply billing*

The Domestic Gas Supply Company records its customers' gas usage figures on a Customer Usage File. Each record on the file contains the customer number, customer name, customer address and gas usage expressed in cubic metres.

The company bills its customers according to the following rate: if the customer's usage is 60 cubic metres or less, a rate of $2.00 per cubic metre is applied; if the customer's usage is more than 60 cubic metres, then a rate of $1.75 per cubic metre is applied for the first 60 cubic metres and $1.50 per cubic metre for the remaining usage.

Design a solution algorithm which will <u>read</u> the Customer Usage File and <u>produce</u> a report listing each customer's number, name, address, gas usage and the amount owing.

At the end of the report, <u>print</u> the total number of customers and the total amount owing to the company.

A   Defining diagram

Input	Processing	Output
customer usage records	Print heading	heading line
• customer_number	Read usage records	customer details
• name	Calculate amount owing	• customer_number
• address	Print customer details	• name
• gas_usage	Compute total customers	• address
	Compute total amount owing	• gas_usage
	Print totals	• amount_owing
		total_customers
		total_amount_owing

B   Control structures required

1   A DOWHILE loop to control the repetition,
2   IF statements to calculate the amount_owing, and
3   Accumulators for total_customers and total_amount_owing.

C   Solution algorithm

```
Bill_gas_customers
    Print 'CUSTOMER USAGE FIGURES' heading
    Set total_customers to zero
    Set total_amount_owing to zero
    Read customer record
    DOWHILE more records
        IF usage ≤ 60 THEN
            amount_owing = usage * $2.00
        ELSE
            amount_owing = (60 * $1.75) + ((usage − 60) * $1.50)
        ENDIF
        Print customer_number, name, address, gas_usage, amount_owing
        Add amount_owing to total_amount_owing
        Add 1 to total_customers
        Read customer record
    ENDDO
    Print total_customers
    Print total_amount_owing
END
```

Note that, in this example, there is:

• initial processing before the loop,
• processing of the current record within the loop, and
• final processing after exiting the loop.

6.2 CHAPTER SUMMARY

This chapter developed solution algorithms to eight typical programming problems. The approach to all eight problems followed the same path:

1 The problem was defined, using a defining diagram.
2 The control structures required were written down, along with any extra variables required.
3 The solution algorithm was produced, using pseudocode and the three basic control structures: sequence, selection and repetition.

It was noted that the solution algorithms mostly followed the same basic pattern, although the statements within the pattern were quite different. This pattern was first introduced in Chapter 5, as follows:

```
Process_sequential_file
    Initial processing
    Read first record
    DOWHILE more records exist
        Process this record
        Read next record
    ENDDO
    Final processing
END
```

6.3 PROGRAMMING PROBLEMS

Construct a solution algorithm for the following programming problems. Your solution should contain:

- a defining diagram,
- a list of control structures required,
- a pseudocode algorithm, and
- a desk check of the algorithm.

1 A parts inventory record contains the following fields.

- record code (only code 11 is valid),
- part number (6 characters; 2 alpha and 4 numeric, e.g. AA1234),
- part description, and
- inventory balance.

Design a program which will read this file of parts inventory records and print the contents of all the valid inventory records that have a zero inventory balance.

2 Design a program which will read the same parts inventory file described in problem 1, and print the details of all valid records whose

part numbers fall within the values AA3000 and AA3999 inclusive. Your program is also required to print a count of these selected records at the end of the parts listing.

3 Design a program which will produce the same report as in problem 2, but will also print, at the end of the parts listing, a count of all the records whose part number begins with the value 'AA' as well as a count of those records whose part numbers fall between AA3000 and AA3999.

4 Design an algorithm which will read an array of 200 characters and display to the screen a count of the occurrences of each of the five vowels (a, e, i, o, u) in the array.

5 An Electricity Supply Authority records its customers' Usage Figures on an Electricity Usage File. This file consists of:

(a) A header record (first record) which provides the total kilowatt hours used during the month, by all customers.

(b) A number of detail records, each containing the customer number, customer name and electricity usage in kilowatt hours for the month.

Design a solution algorithm which will read the Electricity Usage File and produce an 'ELECTRICITY USAGE' report showing the customer's number, name, customer usage figure and amount owing. The amount owing is calculated at 11 cents for each kilowatt hour used up to 200 hours and 8 cents for each kilowatt hour over 200 hours. The total customer usage in kilowatt hours is also to be accumulated.

At the end of the program, compare the total customer usage which was accumulated in the program with the value provided in the header record, and print an appropriate message if the totals are not equal.

6 Design a program which will read a file of customer credit account balances and produce a report showing the customer's minimum amount due. Each customer record contains the customer number, name, address, postcode and total amount owing.

The minimum amount due is calculated to be one quarter of the total amount owing, provided this calculated amount is not less than $5.00. At least $5.00 must be paid when the total amount owing is greater than $5.00. If the total amount owing is $5.00 or less, then the total amount is payable.

7 A file of student records contains name, gender (M or F), age (in years) and marital status (single or married). Design a program to read through the file and compute the numbers of married men, single men, married women and single women. Print these numbers on a 'STUDENT SUMMARY' report. If any single men are over 30 years of age, print their names on a separate 'SINGLE MEN' report.

Modularisation

7.1 MODULARISATION

Throughout the previous chapters it has been emphasised that to design a solution algorithm, you must:

- define the problem,
- write down the control structures required to reach a solution, and
- devise a solution algorithm, which uses a combination of sequence, selection and repetition control structures.

Many solution algorithms have been presented, and all have been relatively simple; that is, the finished algorithm has been less than one page in length. As programming problems increase in complexity, however, it becomes more and more difficult to consider the solution as a whole. Given a complex problem, you often will not be able to see initially what the solution might be. So you must first identify the major tasks to be performed in the problem, and then divide the problem into sections which represent those tasks. These sections can be considered subtasks or functions. Once the major tasks in the problem have been identified you may then need to look at each of the subtasks and identify within them further subtasks, and so on. This process of identifying first the major tasks and then further subtasks within them is known as top-down design, or functional decomposition.

By using this top-down design methodology you are adopting a modular approach to program design. That is, each of the subtasks or functions will eventually become a module within a solution algorithm or program. A module, then, can be defined as a section of an algorithm which is dedicated to a single function. The use of modules makes the algorithm simpler, more systematic, and more likely to be free of errors. Since each module represents a single task, you can develop the solution algorithm task by task, or module by module, until the complete solution has been devised.

Top-down design methodology allows you to concentrate on the overall design of the algorithm without getting too involved with the details of the lower-level modules. Another benefit of top-down design is that separate modules, once identified and written, can be re-used or independently modified if necessary.

The modularisation process

The division of a problem into smaller subtasks, or modules is a relatively simple process. When you are defining the problem, write down the activities or processing steps to be performed. These activities are then grouped together to form more manageable tasks or functions, which will eventually form modules. The emphasis when defining the problem must still be to concentrate on what tasks or functions need to be performed. Each function will be made up of a number of activities, all of which contribute to the performance of a single task.

A module must be large enough to perform its task, and must include only the operations which contribute to the performance of that task. It should have a single entry and a single exit with a top-to-bottom sequence of instructions. The name of the module should describe the work to be done as a single specific function. The convention of naming a module by using a verb followed by a two-word object is particularly important here, as it helps to identify the separate task or function which the module has been designed to perform. Also, the careful naming of modules using this convention makes the algorithm and resultant code easier to follow. For example, typical module names might be:

Print_page_headings
Calculate_sales_tax
Validate_input_date

By using meaningful module names such as these, you can automatically describe the task that the module has been designed to perform, and anyone reading the algorithm can easily see what the module is supposed to do.

The mainline

Since each module performs a single specific task, a mainline routine must provide the master control which ties all the modules together and co-ordinates their activity. This program mainline should show the main processing functions and the order in which they are to be performed. It should also show the flow of data and the major control structures. The mainline should be easy to read, be of manageable length, and show sound logic structure. Generally, you should be able to read a pseudocode mainline and see exactly what is being done in the program.

Let us now look at two algorithms which were introduced in Chapter 4 whose solutions will be much simpler once modularisation is used.

EXAMPLE 7.1   *Read three characters*

Design a solution algorithm which will: prompt a terminal operator for three characters, accept those characters as input, sort them into ascending sequence and output them to the screen. The algorithm is to continue to accept characters until 'XXX' is entered.

A   Defining diagram

Input	Processing	Output
char_1	Prompt for characters	char_1
char_2	Accept three characters	char_2
char_3	Sort three characters	char_3
	Output three characters	

B   Solution algorithm

```
Read_three_characters
      Prompt the operator for char_1, char_2, char_3
      Get char_1, char_2, char_3
      DOWHILE NOT (char_1 = X AND char_2 = X AND char_3 = X)
          IF char_1 > char_2 THEN
              temp = char_1
              char_1 = char_2
              char_2 = temp
          ENDIF
          IF char_2 > char_3 THEN
              temp = char_2
              char_2 = char_3
              char_3 = temp
          ENDIF
          IF char_1 > char_2 THEN
              temp = char_1
              char_1 = char_2
              char_2 = temp
          ENDIF
          Output to the screen char_1, char_2, char_3
          Prompt operator for char_1, char_2, char_3
          Get char_1, char_2, char_3
      ENDDO
END
```

This solution looks cumbersome and awkward, so it is an ideal candidate for modularisation as follows:

C   Solution algorithm using a module

One of the processing steps in the defining diagram is to 'sort three characters'. In the algorithm above, this was converted into three separate IF statements in the mainline. The mainline could have been simplified considerably if these three IF statements were put into a separate module called Sort_three_characters and the module was called by the mainline when required. The module would then perform the single specific task of sorting the three characters into ascending sequence. The solution algorithm would now look like this:

```
Read_three_characters
      Prompt the operator for char_1, char_2, char_3
      Get char_1, char_2, char_3
      DOWHILE NOT (char_1 = X AND char_2 = X AND char_3 = X)
            Sort_three_characters
            Output to the screen char_1, char_2, char_3
            Prompt operator for char_1, char_2, char_3
            Get char_1, char_2, char_3
      ENDDO
END

Sort_three_characters
      IF char_1 > char_2 THEN
            temp = char_1
            char_1 = char_2
            char_2 = temp
      ENDIF
      IF char_2 > char_3 THEN
            temp = char_2
            char_2 = char_3
            char_3 = temp
      ENDIF
      IF char_1 > char_2 THEN
            temp = char_1
            char_1 = char_2
            char_2 = temp
      ENDIF
END
```

The solution algorithm now consists of two modules; a mainline module called Read_three_characters and a submodule called Sort_three_ characters. When the mainline wants to pass control to its submodule, it simply names that module. Control then passes to the called module, and when the processing in that module is complete the module passes control back to the mainline. The resultant mainline is simple and easy to read. The mainline and its module should now be represented in a hierarchy chart.

7.2 | HIERARCHY CHARTS OR STRUCTURE CHARTS

After the tasks have been grouped into functions or modules, you should present these modules graphically in a diagram. This diagram is known as a hierarchy chart, as it shows not only the names of all the modules but also their hierarchical relationship to each other.

A hierarchy chart may also be referred to as a structure chart or a visual table of contents. The hierarchy chart uses a tree-like diagram of boxes; each box represents a module in the program, and the lines connecting the boxes represent the relationship of the modules to others in the program hierarchy. The chart shows no particular sequence for processing the modules, only the modules themselves in the order in which they first appear in the algorithm.

At the top of the hierarchy chart is the controlling module, or mainline. On the next level are the modules which are called directly from the mainline; that is, the modules immediately subordinate to the mainline. On the next level are the modules which are subordinate to the modules on the first level, and so on. This diagrammatic form of hierarchical relationship appears similar to an organisational chart of personnel within a large company.

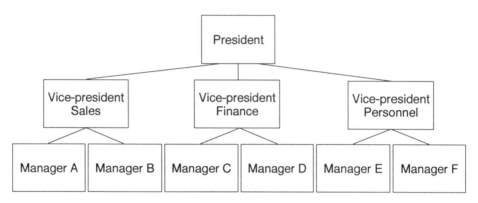

The mainline will pass control to each module when it is ready for that module to perform its task. The controlling module is said to invoke or call the subordinate module. The controlling module is, therefore, referred to as the calling module, and the subordinate module the called module. On completion of its task, the called module returns control to the calling module.

The hierarchy chart for the solution algorithm for Example 7.1 would be relatively simple. It would show a calling module (Read_three_characters) and a called module (Sort_three_characters) as follows:

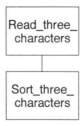

EXAMPLE 7.2 *Calculate employee's pay*

A program is required by a company to <u>read</u> an employee's number, pay rate and the number of hours worked in a week. The program is then to <u>compute</u> the employee's weekly pay and <u>print</u> it along with the input data. The program is to continue <u>reading</u> employee details until there are no more records on the file.

According to the company's rules, no employee may be paid for more than 60 hours per week, and the maximum hourly rate is $25.00 per hour. If more than 35 hours are worked, then payment for the overtime hours worked is calculated at time-and-a-half. If the hours worked field or the hourly rate field is out of range, then the input data and an appropriate message is to be <u>printed</u> and the employee's weekly pay is not to be calculated.

A Defining diagram

Input	Processing	Output
emp_no	Read employee details	emp_no
pay_rate	Validate input fields	pay_rate
hrs_worked	Calculate employee pay	hrs_worked
	Print employee details	emp_weekly_pay
		error_message

B Solution algorithm

```
Compute_employee_pay
    Read emp_no, pay_rate, hrs_worked
    DOWHILE more records
        Set valid_input_fields to true
        Set error_message to blank
        IF pay_rate > $25 THEN
            error_message = 'Pay rate exceeds $25.00'
            valid_input_fields = false
            Print emp_no, pay_rate, hrs_worked, error_message
        ENDIF
        IF hrs_worked > 60 THEN
            error_message = 'Hours worked exceeds limit of 60'
            valid_input_fields = false
            Print emp_no, pay_rate, hrs_worked, error_message
        ENDIF
        IF valid_input_fields THEN
            IF hrs_worked ≤ 35 THEN
                emp_weekly_pay = pay_rate * hrs_worked
            ELSE
                overtime_hrs = hrs_worked – 35
```

```
                        overtime_pay = overtime_hrs * pay_rate * 1.5
                        emp_weekly_pay = (pay_rate * 35) + overtime_pay
                    ENDIF
                    Print emp_no, pay_rate, hrs_worked, emp_weekly_pay
                ENDIF
                Read emp_no, pay_rate, hrs_worked
            ENDDO
        END
```

This solution algorithm, like that for Example 7.1, looks cumbersome, and its readability could be greatly improved by modularisation.

(c) *Solution algorithm using modules.*

There are two separate functions to be performed in this algorithm: the validation of the input data, and the calculation and printing of the employee's pay. The pseudocode for each of these functions could be placed into two separate modules called Validate_input_fields and Calculate_ employee_pay. The variable valid_input_fields will be used as a control flag to control the calculation of the employee's pay. The three modules can be represented by a hierarchy diagram, as follows:

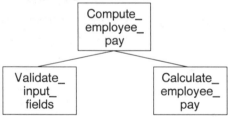

The solution algorithm would then look like this:

```
Compute_employee_pay
    Set valid_input_fields to true
    Read emp_no, pay_rate, hrs_worked
    DOWHILE more records
        Validate_input_fields
        IF valid_input_fields THEN
            Calculate_employee_pay
            Print emp_no, pay_rate, hrs_worked, emp_weekly_pay
        ELSE
            set valid_input_fields to true
        ENDIF
        Read emp_no, pay_rate, hrs_worked
    ENDDO
END
```

```
Validate_input_fields
    Set error_message to blank
    IF pay_rate > $25 THEN
        error_message = 'Pay rate exceeds $25.00'
        valid_input_fields = false
        Print emp_no, pay_rate, hrs_worked, error_message
    ENDIF
    IF hrs_worked > 60 THEN
        error_message = 'Hours worked exceeds limit of 60'
        valid_input_fields = false
        Print emp_no, pay_rate, hrs_worked, error_message
    ENDIF
END

Calculate_employee_pay
    IF hrs_worked ≤ 35 THEN
        emp_weekly_pay = pay_rate * hrs_worked
    ELSE
        overtime_hrs = hrs_worked − 35
        overtime_pay = overtime_hrs * pay_rate * 1.5
        emp_weekly_pay = (pay_rate * 35) + overtime_pay
    ENDIF
END
```

By writing the solution algorithm as three separate modules, the readability of the solution has been dramatically improved. The mainline will invoke its subordinate modules when it wants to pass control to them. Similarly, when processing is complete in the called module, control will pass back to the calling module. By breaking the tasks into smaller, more manageable modules, you can concentrate on the main logic of the mainline, leaving the details of the lower-level modules till later.

EXAMPLE 7.3   *Create patient bill*

Let us look at the pseudocode mainline for a program which produces bills for patients upon their discharge from hospital. The program is named Create_patient_bill and it calls several modules from within the mainline.

```
Create_patient_bill
    Initialise charges fields
    Read patient charges record
    DOWHILE patient records exist
        Compute_accommodation_charges
        Compute_theatre_charges
        Compute_pathology_charges
        Compute_sundries_charges
        Print_patient_bill
        Read patient charges record
    ENDDO
    Print total_patients, total_charges
END
```

This mainline calls on a series of modules to perform the task of generating a hospital patient's bill. The mainline passes control to a module which performs a task. When the module reaches its end, it passes control back to the mainline, which then passes control to the next module, and so on.

Note that the name of each module describes the specific function for which it is intended. Without knowing the contents of any of the modules, you can read this mainline and obtain a good idea of what is happening in the program.

The hierarchy chart for the program Create_patient_bill, as developed so far, looks like this:

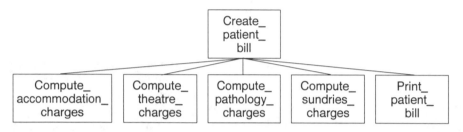

The mainline module Create_patient_bill calls each of its subordinate modules in turn. One of these called modules may itself call other subordinate modules. For instance, the Compute_theatre_charges module may need to call other modules to help it complete its task. It may call, for example, three modules, named Calculate_doctors_charges, Calculate_anaesthetists_charges, and Calculate_facilities_charges.

Similarly, Compute_sundries_charges may need to call two other modules, named Calculate_TV_charges and Calculate_telephone_charges.

When we add these new modules to the next level of the hierarchy chart, it could look like this:

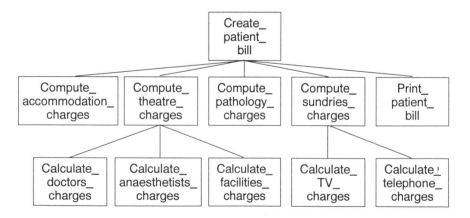

As a rule, no module should have more than seven modules subordinate to it. Using more than seven modules is an indication that you may be considering too many subtasks at once.

7.3 STEPS IN MODULARISATION

Top-down modular design is quite simple if the following steps are performed every time you are presented with a programming problem:

1   Define the problem by dividing it into its three components: input, output and processing. The processing component should consist of a list of activities to be performed.

2   Group the activities into subtasks or functions to determine the modules which will make up the program. Remember that a module is one section of a program dedicated to the performance of a single function. Note that not all the activities may be identified at this stage. Only the modules of the first level of the hierarchy chart may be identified, with other more subordinate modules developed later.

3   Construct a hierarchy chart to illustrate the modules and their relationship to each other. Once the structure (or organisation) of the program has been developed, the order of processing of the modules can be considered.

4   Establish the logic of the mainline of the algorithm in pseudocode. This mainline should contain some initial processing before the loop, some processing within the loop, and some final processing after exiting the loop. It should contain calls to the major processing modules of the program, and should be easy to read and understand.

5   Develop the pseudocode for each successive module in the hierarchy chart. The modularisation process is complete when the pseudocode for each module on the lowest level of the hierarchy chart has been developed.

6   Desk check the solution algorithm. This is achieved by first desk checking the mainline, and then each subordinate module in turn.

7.4 PROGRAMMING EXAMPLES USING MODULES

The solution algorithms to the following programming examples will be developed using the six steps in modularisation introduced in section 7.3.

EXAMPLE 7.4   *Produce orders report*

The Acme Spare Parts Company wants to produce an Orders Report from its Product Orders File. Each record on the file contains the product number of the item ordered, the product description, the number of units ordered, the retail price per unit, the freight charges per unit, and the packaging costs per unit.

The output report is to contain headings and column headings as specified in the following chart:

	ACME SPARE PARTS ORDERS REPORT		PAGE xx
PRODUCT NO	PRODUCT DESCRIPTION	UNITS ORDERED	TOTAL AMOUNT DUE
xxxx	xxxxxxxxxxx	xxx	xxxxx
xxxx	xxxxxxxxxxx	xxx	xxxxx

Each detail line is to contain the product number, description, number of units ordered and the total amount due for the order. There is to be an allowance of 45 detail lines per page.

The amount due for each product is the number of units ordered times the retail price of the unit. A discount of 10% is allowed on the amount due for all orders over $100.00. The freight charges and packaging costs per unit must be added to this resulting value to determine the total amount due.

A   *Define the problem*

Input	Processing	Output
Order record	Print headings as required	main headings
• prod_number	Read order records	column headings
• prod_description	Calculate amount due	page number
• no_of_units	Calculate discount	detail lines
• retail_price	Calculate freight charge	• prod_number
• freight_charge	Calculate packaging	• prod_description
• packaging_cost	Print order details	• no_of_units
	Compute page increments	• total_amount_due

B   *Group the activities into modules*

The activities in the processing component can be grouped into two functions or modules, as follows:

1   'Print headings as required' can become a module. This is an example of

a module which will be created because it is re-usable. That is, the module will be called whenever the report needs to skip to a new page. A page headings module is a standard requirement of most report programs. The name of this module will be Print_page_headings.

2 The four processing steps:

- calculate amount due,
- calculate discount,
- calculate freight charge, and
- calculate packaging,

can be grouped together because they all contribute to the performance of a single task: to calculate the total_amount_due. It is this total_amount_due which is required on each detail line of the report. The name of this module will be Calculate_total_amount_due to describe its function.

C Construct a hierarchy chart

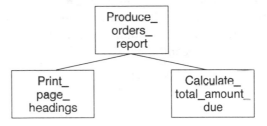

This diagram illustrates the structure of the algorithm. The main controlling module, or mainline, is called 'Produce_orders_report'. The mainline will call on two subordinate modules, namely 'Print_page_headings' and 'Calculate_total_amount_due', as required. When the mainline calls on a module, it will pass control to that module. All the processing steps in that module will then be executed before control returns to the mainline.

D Establish the logic of the mainline of the algorithm. Express the solution algorithm using pseudocode

The mainline will require:

1 A DOWHILE loop to control the repetition,
2 Calls to its two subordinate modules,
3 A page accumulator for the page heading routine, and
4 A line counter to record the number of detail lines printed on each page.

```
Produce_orders_report
      Set page_counter to zero
      Print_page_headings
      Set line_counter to zero
      Read order record
      DOWHILE more records
            IF line_counter ≥ 45 THEN
                  Print_page_headings
                  Set line_counter to zero
            ENDIF
            Calculate_total_amount_due
            Print prod_number, prod_description, no_of_units, total_amount_due
            Add 1 to line_counter
            Read order record
      ENDDO
END
```

E   Develop pseudocode for each successive module in the hierarchy chart

1   The pseudocode for 'Print_page_headings' is standard for a page heading routine which will increment the page counter and print a series of headings. You can assume that the page counter will be printed on one of the main heading lines.

```
Print_page_headings
      Add 1 to page_counter
      Print main headings 'ACME SPARE PARTS'
      Print heading 'ORDERS REPORT'
      Print column headings 1
      Print column headings 2
      Print blank line
END
```

2   The pseudocode for the module 'Calculate_total_amount_due' will compute the total amount due using a series of intermediate calculations.

```
Calculate_total_amount_due
      amount_due = no_of_units * retail_price
      IF amount_due > $100.00 THEN
            discount = amount_due * 0.1
      ELSE
            discount = zero
      ENDIF
      amount_due = amount_due – discount
      freight_due = freight_charge * no_of_units
      packaging_due = packaging_charge * no_of_units
      total_amount_due = amount_due + freight_due + packaging_due
END
```

F Desk check the solution algorithm

The desk checking of an algorithm with modules is no different to the method developed for our previous examples:

1 Create some valid input test data.
2 List the output that the input data is expected to produce.
3 Use a desk check table to walk the data through the mainline of the algorithm to ensure that the expected output is achieved.

In this example, the two subordinate modules consist merely of a series of sequential statements; there is no need to desk check the modules individually, as they can be desk checked at the same time as the mainline. However, if a module contains logic which is particularly complicated, then a separate desk check table should be drawn up for that module as well as the mainline module.

(i) Input data:
Three test cases will be used to test the algorithm. To test for correct page skipping, you can temporarily reduce the line limit from 45 to a conveniently small number, e.g. 2.

Record	prod_ no	prod_ description	no_of_ units	retail_ price	freight_ charge	packaging_ charge
1	100	rubber hose	10	1.00	0.20	0.50
2	200	steel pipe	20	2.00	0.10	0.20
3	300	steel bolt	100	3.00	0.10	0.20
EOF						

(ii) Expected results:

```
                    ACME SPARE PARTS          PAGE 1
                     ORDERS REPORT

     PRODUCT         PRODUCT          UNITS        TOTAL AMOUNT
        NO         DESCRIPTION       ORDERED           DUE

       100         Rubber Hose         10            $17.00
       200         Steel Pipe          20            $40.00
       300         Steel Bolt         100           $300.00
```

(iii) Desk check table:

Only the processing steps of the mainline of the algorithm will be written down in the desk check table. When a call is made to a module, all the processing steps in that module will be recorded on one line of the desk check table. By doing this, the internal logic of each module is checked at the same time as that of the mainline.

Statement	DOWHILE OK?	page_ counter	line_ counter	prod_ no	no_of_ units	retail_ price	freight_ charge	packaging_ charge	total_ amount_ due
Initialise		0							
Print_page_headings		1							
Initialise			0						
Read				100	10	1.00	0.20	0.50	
DOWHILE	yes								
IF									
Calculate									17.00
Print				print	print				print
Add			1						
Read				200	20	2.00	0.10	0.20	
DOWHILE	yes								
IF									
Calculate									46.00
Print				print	print				print
Add			2						
Read				300	100	3.00	0.10	0.20	
DOWHILE	yes								
IF									
Calculate									300.00
Print				print	print				print
Add			3						
Read				EOF					
DOWHILE	no								
END									

EXAMPLE 7.5 *Calculate vehicle registration costs*

A program is required to calculate and print the registration cost of a new vehicle that a customer has ordered.

The program is to be interactive. That is, all the input details will be provided at a terminal on the salesperson's desk. The program will then calculate the related costs and return the information to the screen.

The input details required are:

> Owner's name
> Vehicle make
> Vehicle model
> Weight (in kg)
> Body type (sedan or wagon)
> Private or business code ('P' or 'B')
> Wholesale price of vehicle

A federal tax is also to be paid. This is calculated at the rate of $2.00 for each $100.00, or part thereof, of the wholesale price of the vehicle.

The vehicle registration cost is calculated as the sum of the following charges:

Registration fee	$27.00	
Tax levy	PRIVATE	5% of wholesale price
	BUSINESS	7% of wholesale price
Weight tax	PRIVATE	1% of weight (converted to $)
	BUSINESS	3% of weight (converted to $)
Insurance premium	PRIVATE	1% of wholesale price
	BUSINESS	2% of wholesale price

The program is to calculate the total registration charges for the vehicle plus federal tax, and is to print all the relevant information on the screen as follows:

> Vehicle make:
> Vehicle model:
> Body type:
> Registration fee:
> Tax levy:
> Weight tax:
> Insurance premium:
> Total registration charges:
> Federal tax:
> Total amount payable:

(Total amount payable = total registration charges + federal tax.)

The program is to process registration costs until an owner's name of 'XXX' is entered. None of the other entry details will be required after the value 'XXX' has been entered.

A   Define the problem

Input	Processing	Output
owners_name	Get input details	vehicle_make
vehicle_make	Calculate tax_levy	vehicle_model
vehicle_model	Calculate weight_tax	body_type
weight	Calculate insurance_premium	registration_fee
body_type	Calculate total_registration_costs	tax_levy
usage_code	Calculate federal_tax	weight_tax
wholesale_price	Calculate total_amount_payable	insurance_premium
	Display details to screen	total_registration_charges
		federal_tax
		total_amount_payable

B   Group the activities into modules

The activities in the processing component can be grouped into three main functions, as follows:

1   Get input details.
    There are a number of input fields to read from the screen, so a module can be created to perform this function. The name of the module will be Get_vehicle_details. Note that the read from the screen of the owner's name must be separate, as it is the entry of 'XXX' in this field which will cause the repetition to cease.

2   Display information to screen.
    Similarly, there are a number of output fields to display onto the screen, so a module can be created to perform this function. The name of this module will be Display_registration_details.

3   The following activities in the processing section of the algorithm all contribute to the performance of a single task: to calculate the total amount payable. The name of this module will be Calculate_total_amount_payable.

    • calculate tax_levy,
    • calculate weight_tax,
    • calculate insurance_premium,
    • calculate total_registration_charges,
    • calculate federal_tax, and
    • calculate total_amount_payable.

    To aid readability this module can be divided into two smaller tasks, Calculate_federal_tax and Calculate_total_registration. The module Calculate_total_amount_payable will call these two modules as required to perform those functions.

C   Construct a hierarchy chart

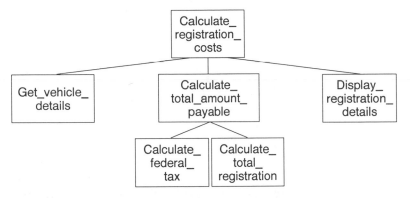

The hierarchy chart illustrates the structure that the algorithm will take. The mainline is called Calculate_registration_costs. It will call three subordinate modules: Get_vehicle_details, Calculate_total_amount_ payable and Display_registration_details. The module Calculate_total_amount_ payable will also call two modules to help perform its task: Calculate_ federal_tax and Calculate_total_registration.

D   Establish the logic of the mainline of the algorithm using pseudocode

The mainline will require:

1   A DOWHILE loop to process the repetition; and
2   Calls to the modules as required.

```
Calculate_registration_costs
     Read owners_name
     DOWHILE owners_name NOT = 'XXX'
          Get_vehicle_details
          Calculate_total_amount_payable
          Display_registration_details
          Read owners_name
     ENDDO
END
```

The mainline appears to be very simple. It consists of a Read before the loop, calls to its three subordinate modules within the loop, and a Read just before the end of the loop. By reading the algorithm, you can easily understand the processing of the program because of the modular nature of the algorithm and the careful choice of module names.

E   Develop the pseudocode for each successive module in the hierarchy chart

1   Get_vehicle_details is a module which prompts for and reads the required fields. The owner's name is read separately in the mainline.

```
Get_vehicle_details
    Get vehicle_make
    Get vehicle_model
    Get weight
    Get body_type
    Get usage_code
    Get wholesale_price
END
```

2   Calculate_total_amount_payable is a module which calls two other modules.

```
Calculate_total_amount_payable
    Calculate_federal_tax
    Calculate_total_registration
    total_amount_payable = federal_tax + total_registration_charges
END
```

3   Calculate_federal_tax contains the steps required to calculate the federal tax. The federal tax is payable at the rate of $2.00 for each $100.00 or part thereof of the wholesale price of the car. (A variable called tax_units is used to count the number of whole $100 units.)

```
Calculate_federal_tax
    Set tax_units = zero
    DOWHILE wholesale_price > $100
        wholesale_price = wholesale_price − 100
        increment tax_units by 1
    ENDDO
    federal_tax = (tax_units + 1) * $2.00
END
```

4   Calculate_total_registration contains all the processing required to calculate the total registration costs. The total cost of registration is the sum of the registration fee, tax levy, weight tax and insurance premium.

```
Calculate_total_registration
    registration_fee = $27.00
    IF usage_code = 'P' THEN
        tax_levy = wholesale_price * 0.05
        weight_tax = weight * 0.01
        insurance_premium = wholesale_price * 0.01
    ELSE
```

```
        tax_levy = wholesale_price * 0.07
        weight_tax = weight * 0.03
        insurance_premium = wholesale_price * 0.02
    ENDIF
    total_registration_charges = registration_fee + tax_levy +
                        weight_tax + insurance_premium
END
```

5 Display_registration_details is a module which displays the required output onto the screen.

```
Display_registration_details
    Display vehicle_make,
    Display vehicle_model,
    Display body_type
    Display registration_fee
    Display tax_levy
    Display weight_tax
    Display insurance_premium
    Display total_registration_charges
    Display federal_tax
    Display total_amount_payable
END
```

When a program is modularised in this fashion, the pseudocode for each successive module becomes very simple.

F *Desk check the solution algorithm*

(i) Input data:

As there are two branches in the logic of the program, two test cases should be sufficient to test the algorithm. Only the relevant input fields will be provided.

Record	weight	usage_code	wholesale_price
1	1000	P	30 000
2	2000	B	20 000
XXX			

(ii) Expected Results:

	Record 1	Record 2
Registration fee	27.00	27.00
Tax levy	1500.00	1400.00
Weight tax	10.00	60.00
Insurance premium	300.00	400.00
Total registration charges	1837.00	1887.00
Federal tax	600.00	400.00
Total amount payable	2437.00	2287.00

(iii) Desk Check Table:

The desk checking will be of the main processing steps of the mainline. When a call to a module is made, all the processing steps of the module are recorded on one line of the desk check table. This, in effect, checks both the mainline logic and the modules at the same time.

Statement	owners name	DOWHILE OK?	weight	usage_ code	wholesale_ price	federal_ tax	total_ registration	total_ amount_ payable
Initialise								0
Read	1							
DOWHILE		yes						
Get			1000	P	30 000			
Calculate						600	1837	2437
Display						yes	yes	yes
Read	2							
DOWHILE		yes						
Get			2000	B	20 000			
Calculate						400	1887	2287
Display						yes	yes	yes
Read	XXX							
DOWHILE		no						
END								

7.5 CHAPTER SUMMARY

This chapter introduced a modular approach to program design. The terms 'top-down design' and 'module' were defined, and programming examples were provided to show the benefits of using modularisation.

Hierarchy charts were introduced as a method of illustrating the structure of a program which contains modules. Hierarchy charts show the names of all the modules and their hierarchical relationship to each other.

The steps in modularisation which a programmer must follow were listed. These were: define the problem; group the activities into subtasks or functions; construct a hierarchy chart; establish the logic of the mainline; develop the pseudocode for each successive module; and desk check the solution algorithm.

Programming examples which used these six steps in modularisation were then developed in pseudocode.

7.6 PROGRAMMING PROBLEMS

Construct a solution algorithm for the following programming problems. To obtain your final solution you should:

- define the problem,
- group the activities into modules,
- construct a hierarchy chart,
- establish the logic of the mainline using pseudocode,
- develop the pseudocode for each successive module in the hierarchy chart, and
- desk check the solution algorithm.

1 Design an algorithm which will prompt for and receive your current cheque book balance, followed by a number of financial transactions. Each transaction consists of a transaction code and a transaction amount. The transaction code can be a deposit ('D') or a cheque ('C'). After each transaction has been processed, a new balance is to be displayed on the screen, with a warning message if the balance becomes negative. When there are no more transactions, a 'Q' transaction code is to be entered to signify the end of the data. Your algorithm is then to display the initial and final balances, along with a count of the number of cheques and deposits processed.

2 The members of the Board of a small university are considering voting for a pay increase for their 25 faculty members. They are considering a pay increase of 8%, but before doing so they want to know how much this pay increase will cost. Design an algorithm which will prompt for and accept the current salary for each of the faculty members, and then calculate and display their individual pay increases. At the end of the algorithm, you are to print the total faculty payroll before and after the pay increase, and the total pay increase involved.

3 The Tidy Phones Telephone Company's charges file contains records for each call made by its Metroville subscribers during a month. Each record on the file contains: the subscriber's name, subscriber's phone number, phone number called, distance from Metroville of the number called (in kilometres), and the duration of the call (in seconds).

Design a program which will read the Tidy Phones charges file and produce a Telephone Charges report, as follows:

```
                        TIDY PHONES              PAGE xx
                     TELEPHONE CHARGES

SUBSCRIBER      SUBSCRIBER      PHONE NUMBER        COST OF
   NAME           NUMBER          CALLED             CALL
   xxxx         xxxxxxxxxxx      xxx-xxxx            999.99
   xxxx         xxxxxxxxxxx      xxx-xxxx            999.99

                                 TOTAL REVENUE      9999.99
```

Main headings and column headings are to appear as printed on the report with an allowance of 45 detail lines per page. The Total Revenue line is to print three lines after the last detail line.

The cost of each call is calculated as follows:

Distance from Metroville	Cost ($)/Minute
less than 25 km	0.35
25 ≤ km < 75	0.65
75 ≤ km < 300	1.00
300 ≤ km ≤ 1000	2.00
greater than 1000 km	3.00

4   The Mitre-11 hardware outlets require an inventory control program which is to accept order details for an item, and generate a Shipping List and a Back Order List.

Design an interactive program which will conduct a dialogue on the screen for the input values, and print two reports as required. The screen dialogue is to appear as follows:

```
ENTER Item No      :   99999
Quantity on Hand   :   999
Order quantity     :   999
Order number       :   999999
```

If an item number does not have precisely five digits then an error message is to appear on the screen.

If the quantity on hand is sufficient to meet the order then one line is to be printed on the Shipping List.

If the quantity on hand is insufficient to meet the order, then the order is to be partially filled by whatever stock is available. For this situation, one line should appear on the Shipping List with the appropriate number of units shipped and a message 'Order Partially Filled'. An entry for the balance of the order is to be printed on the Back Order List.

If the quantity on hand is zero, then the message 'OUT OF STOCK' is to appear on the Shipping List, and an entry for the full quantity ordered is to be printed on the Back Order List.

Your program is to continue to process inventory orders until a value of zero is entered for the item number.

Report layouts for the Shipping List and Back Order List are as follows:

```
                    MITRE–11 HARDWARE        PAGE xx
                    INVENTORY CONTROL
                      SHIPPING LIST

   ORDER            ITEM              UNITS          MESSAGE
    NO               NO              SHIPPED

   999999          99999              999              —
   999999          99999              999              —
```

```
                    MITRE–11 HARDWARE        PAGE xx
                    INVENTORY CONTROL
                     BACK ORDER LIST

      ORDER            ITEM          BACK ORDER
       NO               NO              QTY

      999999          99999             999
      999999          99999             999
```

Communication between modules

You never pass parameters with me anymore

8.1 PROGRAM DATA

In the first seven chapters, the main emphasis has been the development of the solution algorithm. Many examples have been given which define the problem, break the problem into appropriate modules, establish the control structures required, develop the solution algorithm and desk check the solution.

However, because programs are written to process data, you must also have a good understanding of the nature and structure of the data being processed. Data within a program may be a single variable, such as an integer or a character, or a group item (sometimes called an aggregate) such as an array or a file.

Variables, constants and literals

A variable is the name given to a collection of memory cells designed to store a particular data item. It is called a variable because the value stored in that variable may change or vary as the program executes. For example, the variable total_amount may contain several values during the execution of the program.

A constant is a data item with a name and value which remains the same during the execution of the program. For example, the name 'fifty' may be given to a data item which contains the value 50.

A literal is a constant whose name is the written representation of its value. For example, the program may contain the literal '50'.

Elementary data items

An elementary data item is one which contains a single variable that is always treated as a unit. These data items are usually classified into data types. A data type consists of a set of data values and a set of operations which can be performed on those values. The most common elementary data types are:

integer:
    representing a set of whole numbers, positive or negative
real:
    representing a set of numbers, positive or negative, which may include values before or after a decimal point
character:
    representing the set of characters of the alphabet, plus some special characters
Boolean:
    representing a control flag or switch which may contain one of two possible values — true or false.

Data structures

A data structure is an aggregate of other data items. The data items that it contains are its components, which may be elementary data items or another data structure. In a data structure, data is grouped together in a particular way, which reflects the situation with which the program is concerned. The most common data structures are:

record:
> a collection of data items or fields which all bear some relationship to one another. For example, a student record may contain the student's number, name, address, enrolled subjects, etc.

file:
> a collection of records. For example, a student file may contain a collection of the above student records.

array:
> a data structure, which is made up of a number of variables or data items which all have the same data type and are accessed by the same name. For example, an array called scores may contain a collection of students' exam scores. Access to the individual items in the array is made by naming the element of the array; e.g. scores(3).

string:
> a collection of characters. For example, the string 'Jenny Parker' may represent a student's name.

8.2 COMMUNICATION BETWEEN MODULES

When designing solution algorithms, you should consider not only the breaking up of the problem into modules, but also the flow of information between the modules. The fewer and simpler the communications between modules, the easier it is to understand and maintain one module without reference to other modules. This flow of information, called inter-module communication, can be accomplished by using global data or a parameter list.

Global data

In all our examples, information or data has been passed from one module to another by using the same variable names in both the calling module and the called modules of a program. This data is known as global data, because it is known to the whole world of the program and the data can be accessed by every module in the program. All data, however, does not need to be global.

Local data

Variables which are defined within a subordinate module are called local variables. These local variables are not known to the calling module, nor to any other module. Using local variables can reduce what are known as program side effects.

Scope of data

The scope of a variable is the portion of a program in which that variable has been defined and can be referred to. If a list is created of all the modules in which a variable can be referenced, then that list defines the scope of the variable. Thus, the scope of a global variable is the whole program, and the scope of a local variable is simply the module in which it is defined.

Side effects

A side effect is a form of cross-communication of a module with other parts of a program. It occurs when a subordinate module alters the value of a global variable inside a module. Side effects are not necessarily detrimental. However, they do tend to decrease the manageability of a program and you should be aware of their impact.

If a program is amended at any time by a programmer other than the person who wrote it, a change may be made to a global variable. This change could cause side effects or erroneous results because the second programmer is unaware of other modules which also alter that global variable.

Passing parameters

Another method of inter-module communication is the passing of parameters or arguments between modules. A parameter can be a variable, literal, or constant which can communicate between various parts of a program. It may have one of three functions:

1   To pass information from a calling module to a subordinate module. The subordinate module would then use that information in its processing, but would not need to communicate any information back to the calling module.
2   To pass information from a subordinate module to its calling module. The calling module would then use that parameter in subsequent processing.
3   To fulfil a two-way communication role. Information may be passed by the calling module to a subordinate module, where it is amended in some fashion and then passed back to the calling module.

These parameters which pass between modules can be incorporated into a hierarchy chart or structure chart using the following symbols:

for data parameters   for status parameters

Data parameters contain the actual variables or data items which will be passed between modules.

Status parameters act as program flags and should contain just one of two values: true or false. These program flags or switches are set to true or false according to a specific set of conditions. They are then used to control further processing.

When designing modular programs, avoid using data parameters to also indicate status, because this can affect the program in two ways:

1   It may confuse the reader of the program because a variable has been overloaded; i.e. it has been used for more than one purpose; and

2   It may cause unpredictable errors when the program is amended at some later date, as a maintenance programmer may be unaware of the dual purpose of the variable.

8.3   USING PARAMETERS IN PROGRAM DESIGN

Let us look again at Example 7.1 from Chapter 7, but change the solution algorithm so that data parameters are used to communicate between modules.

EXAMPLE 8.1   *Read three characters*

Design a solution algorithm which will <u>prompt</u> a terminal operator for three characters, <u>accept</u> those characters as input, <u>sort</u> them into ascending sequence and <u>output</u> them to the screen. The algorithm is to continue to <u>accept</u> characters until 'XXX' is entered.

A   *Defining diagram*

Input	Processing	Output
char_1	Prompt for characters	char_1
char_2	Accept three characters	char_2
char_3	Sort three characters	char_3
	Output three characters	

B   Group the activities into modules

The activities can be grouped into two main functions:

1   Read_three_characters
2   Sort_three_characters

The module Read_three_characters will send the three input characters to its subordinate module, Sort_three_characters, in the form of parameters. The module Sort_three_characters will then sort the three characters and send these sorted values back to the mainline module as parameters.

C   Construct a hierarchy chart

The hierarchy chart will show not only the modules and their relationship to each other, but also the parameters which are to be passed between the modules.

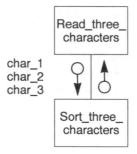

D   Establish the logic of the solution algorithm using pseudocode (mainline and subordinate module)

Parameters are represented in pseudocode as variables within curved brackets. When the mainline calls its subordinate module, it must also list in brackets the parameters it will be sending and receiving. Similarly, the called module will list in brackets the parameters that it will receive and then return to the calling module. The parameters passed in this example will be the three characters: char_1, char_2 and char_3.

```
Read_three_characters
     Prompt the operator for char_1, char_2, char_3
     Get char_1, char_2, char_3
     DOWHILE NOT (char_1 = X AND char_2 = X AND char_3 = X)
          Sort_three_characters (char_1, char_2, char_3)
          Output to the screen char_1, char_2, char_3
          Prompt operator for char_1, char_2, char_3
          Get char_1, char_2, char_3
     ENDDO
END
```

```
Sort_three_characters (char_1, char_2, char_3)
    IF char_1 > char_2 THEN
        temp = char_1
        char_1 = char_2
        char_2 = temp
    ENDIF
    IF char_2 > char_3 THEN
        temp = char_2
        char_2 = char_3
        char_3 = temp
    ENDIF
    IF char_1 > char_2 THEN
        temp = char_1
        char_1 = char_2
        char_2 = temp
    ENDIF
END
```

Let us look again at Example 7.2 from Chapter 7, but change the solution algorithm so that a status parameter is used to communicate between modules.

EXAMPLE 8.2   Calculate employee's pay

A program is required by a company to <u>read</u> an employee's number, pay rate and the number of hours worked in a week. The program is then to <u>compute</u> the employee's weekly pay and <u>print</u> it along with the input data. The program is to continue <u>reading</u> employee details until there are no more records on the file.

According to the company's rules, no employee may be paid for more than 60 hours per week, and the maximum hourly rate is $25.00 per hour. If more than 35 hours are worked, then payment for the overtime hours worked is calculated at time-and-a-half. If the hours worked field or the hourly rate field is out of range, then the input data and an appropriate message is to be <u>printed</u> and the employee's weekly pay is not to be calculated.

A   Defining diagram

Input	Processing	Output
emp_no	Read employee details	emp_no
pay_rate	Validate input fields	pay_rate
hrs_worked	Calculate employee pay	hrs_worked
	Print employee details	emp_weekly_pay
		error_message

B   Group the activities into modules

The activities can be grouped into three main functions:

1   Compute_employee_pay
2   Validate_input_fields
3   Calculate_employee_pay

The mainline Compute_employee_pay will communicate with the module Validate_input_fields by sending a status parameter called valid_input_fields. The module Validate_input_fields will, after validating the input fields, then return the status parameter to the mainline.

C   Construct a hierarchy chart

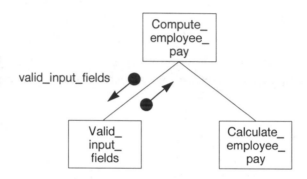

D   Establish the logic of the solution algorithm using pseudocode (mainline and subordinate modules)

```
Compute_employee_pay
    Set valid_input_fields to true
    Read emp_no, pay_rate, hrs_worked
    DOWHILE more records
        Validate_input_fields (valid_input_fields)
        IF valid_input_fields THEN
            Calculate_employee_pay
            Print emp_no, pay_rate, hrs_worked, emp_weekly_pay
        ELSE
            set valid_input_fields to true
        ENDIF
        Read emp_no, pay_rate, hrs_worked
    ENDDO
END

Validate_input_fields (valid_input_fields)
    Set error_message to blank
    IF pay_rate > $25 THEN
        error_message = 'Pay rate exceeds $25.00'
        Print emp_no, pay_rate, hrs_worked, error_message
        valid_input_fields = false
```

```
        ENDIF
        IF hrs_worked > 60 THEN
            error_message = 'Hours worked exceeds limit of 60'
            Print emp_no, pay_rate, hrs_worked, error_message
            valid_input_fields = false
        ENDIF
END

Calculate_employee_pay
        IF hrs_worked ≤ 35 THEN
            emp_weekly_pay = pay_rate * hrs_worked
        ELSE
            overtime_hrs = hrs_worked − 35
            overtime_pay = overtime_hrs * pay_rate * 1.5
            emp_weekly_pay = (pay_rate * 35) + overtime_pay
        ENDIF
END
```

8.4 OBJECT-ORIENTED DESIGN

Throughout this book it has been emphasised that a you must concentrate on what the program is supposed to do, rather than how to do it. If the program is complex, you must break the problem into smaller, more manageable tasks or functions while still concentrating on the overall solution. This design methodology is called top-down design.

Object-oriented design also involves the process of breaking up a complex problem into smaller, simpler components. However, these components are often designed and tested independently of the program which will use them. The two design methodologies differ in that in object-oriented design the system is viewed as a collection of interacting objects rather than functions.

Objects

An object can be considered as a container for a set of data values and a set of operations to be performed on it. Thus, an object can be defined as having the following properties:

1   It has a name.
2   It has a prescribed set of values; sometimes these values can be structured so that the object is viewed as having multiple attributes.
3   There exists a set of operations to be performed on it; often these operations can be interrelated by a set of rules or axioms.

In practical terms, an object will be a data structure which has been defined in conjunction with its set of operations. For example, a program needing to make use of an index, may treat the index as an object. The index will be defined by:

1   a set of values; each value may be comprised of a 'key' (i.e. what you look up) and an 'address' (i.e. where to find it); and

2   a set of operations; operations which can be performed on the index, such as: to look up an address, given a key; to add an entry (i.e. a 'key, address' pair); and to remove an entry.

The main advantage of viewing the index as an object in a program is that the functioning of the index is independent of any data structure used to represent it. It is also independent of any procedures used to implement operations on it.

In object-oriented design, a system can be viewed as a series of modules which operate on objects, without any regard to how the objects are actually built, or how their operations are carried out. An essential feature of object-oriented design is that an object does not need to know how other objects are defined. All that one object may know of another, is of its existence, and the interface between them i.e. the form and meaning of the messages or parameters passed from one to the other. This includes the program itself and all its subordinate modules.

Information hiding

In object-oriented design, the object's internal structure is hidden from the user. This principle is called 'information hiding', a concept first introduced by Parnas[1] in 1972. Information hiding simplifies the use of objects, because you do not need to understand the internal structure of the object, or its operation. You can concentrate on the workings of the module and the communications which that module will have with others in the program via parameters. Other terms related to information hiding are 'data encapsulation' and 'data abstraction'.

Object-oriented design can impose some restrictions when you are designing modules:

1   the individual modules must be completely self-contained and must not depend on the operation of any other sections of the program, and

2   all shared or global data must be eliminated, as communications between objects is only via message passing or parameters.

It is not the intention of this book to delve deeply into examples which use object-oriented design, as this methodology is usually confined to very large and complex problems. However, it is important that you are familiar with the terms used with this methodology and understand the basic concepts behind it.

[1] D. Parnas, 'On the criteria to be used in decomposing systems into modules'. *Comm. ACM* 15 (2), pp. 1053–8 (1972).

8.5 **CHAPTER SUMMARY**

This chapter defined data variables, constants and literals and described the differences between elementary data items and data structures.

Inter-module communication was defined as the flow of information or data between modules. Local and global variables were introduced, along with the scope of a variable and the side effect of using only global data.

Parameters were introduced as a method of communication between modules. A method of representing parameters on a structure chart was devised and two programming examples which used parameters were developed.

Object-oriented design was introduced as another method of approaching a programming problem. This design methodology uses the concept of the system being viewed as a collection of interacting objects whose internal structure is hidden from the user.

8.6 **PROGRAMMING PROBLEMS**

Construct a solution algorithm for each of the following programming problems. Each solution algorithm should be designed so that parameters are passed between modules to provide greater module independence.

To obtain your final solution, you should:

- define the problem,
- group the activities into modules (also consider the data which each module requires),
- construct a hierarchy chart,
- establish the logic of the mainline using pseudocode,
- develop the pseudocode for each successive module in the hierarchy chart, and
- desk check the solution algorithm.

1 Design a program which will prompt for and accept an employee's annual salary and calculate the annual income tax due on that salary. Income tax is calculated according to the following table and is to be displayed on the screen.

Portion of salary	Income tax rate (%)
0 to < 5,000	0
5,000 to < 10,000	6
10,000 to < 20,000	15
20,000 to < 30,000	20
30,000 to < 40,000	25
40,000 and above	30

2   Design a program which will prompt for and accept four numbers, sort
    them into ascending sequence and display them to the screen. Your
    algorithm is to include a module called Order_two_numbers which is to
    be called from the mainline to sort two numbers at a time.

3   Design a program which will prompt for and accept a four-digit
    representation of the year (e.g. 1992). The program is to determine if the
    year provided is a leap year and to print a message to this effect on the
    screen. A message is also to be printed on the screen if the value
    provided is not exactly four numeric digits.

4   Design a program which will read a file of sales volume records and print
    a report showing the sales commission owing to each salesperson. Each
    input record contains salesperson number, name and their volume of
    sales for the month. The commission rate varies according to sales
    volume as follows:

On sales volume ($) of...	Commission rate (%)
0 – 199	5
200 – 999	8
1000 – 1999	10
2000 and above	12

The calculated commission may be a combination of amounts according to
the sales volume figure. For example, the commission owing for a sales
volume of $1200 would be calculated as follows:

Commission = (200 * 5) + ((1000 − 200) * 8) + ((1200 − 1000) * 10))

Your program is to print the salesperson number, name, their volume of
sales and their calculated commission, with the appropriate column
headings.

Cohesion and coupling

MODULE COHESION

A module has been defined as a section of an algorithm which is dedicated to the performance of a single function. It contains a single entry and a single exit, and the name chosen for the module should describe its function.

Programmers often need guidance in determining what makes a good module. Common queries are 'How big should a module be?', 'Is this module too small?' or 'Should I put all the read statements in one module?'

There is a method you can use to remove some of the guesswork when establishing modules. You can look at the cohesion of the module. Cohesion is a measure of the internal strength of a module, i.e. how closely the elements or statements of a module are associated with each other. The more closely the elements of a module are associated, the higher the cohesion of the module. Modules with high cohesion are considered good modules, because of their internal strength.

Edward Yourdon and Larry Constantine[1] established seven levels of cohesion and placed them in a scale from the weakest to the strongest.

Cohesion level	Cohesion attribute	Resultant module strength
Coincidental	Low Cohesion	Weakest
Logical		
Temporal		
Procedural		
Communicational		
Sequential		
Functional	High Cohesion	Strongest

Each level of cohesion in the table will be discussed in this chapter, and pseudocode examples which illustrate each level will also be provided.

Coincidental cohesion

The weakest form of cohesion a module can have is coincidental cohesion. It occurs when elements are collected into a module simply because they happen to fall together. There is no meaningful relationship between the elements at all, and so it is difficult to concisely define the function of the module.

[1] Edward Yourdon & Larry Constantine, *Structured Design: Fundamentals of a Discipline of Computer Program and System Design*. Prentice-Hall, 1979.

Fortunately, these types of modules are rare in today's programming practice. They typically used to occur as a result of one of the following conditions:

- an existing program may have been arbitrarily segmented into smaller modules because of hardware constrictions on the operation of the program;
- existing modules may have been arbitrarily subdivided to conform to a badly considered programming standard (for example, each module should have no more than 50 program statements);
- a number of existing modules may have been combined into one module to either reduce the number of modules in a program or to increase the number of statements in a module to a particular minimum number.

With continually increasing storage capacity and speed of execution, modules which are forced to contain unrelated elements for the above reasons occur only rarely.

Here is a pseudocode example of a module which has coincidental cohesion:

```
File_processing
     Open employee updates file
     Read employee record
     Print_page_headings
     Open employee master file
     Set page_count to one
     Set error_flag to false
END
```

Notice that the instructions within the module have no meaningful relationship to each other.

Logical cohesion

Logical cohesion occurs when the elements of a module are grouped together according to a certain class of activity. That is, the elements fall into some general category because they all do the same kind of thing.

An example might be a module which performs all the read statements for three different files: a sort of 'Read_all_files' module. In such a case the calling module would need to indicate which of the three files it required the called module to read, by sending a parameter.

A module such as this is slightly stronger than a coincidentally cohesive module, because the elements are, at least, somewhat related. However, logically cohesive modules are usually made up of a number of smaller, independent sections, which should exist independently rather than be combined together because of a related activity. Often when a module such as this is called, only a small subset of the elements within the module will be executed.

A pseudocode example for a 'Read_all_files' module might look like this:

```
Read_all_files (file_code)
      CASE of file_code
      1 :   Read customer transaction record
            IF not EOF
                increment customer_transaction_count
            ENDIF
      2 :   Read customer master record
            IF not EOF
                increment customer_master_count
            ENDIF
      3 :   Read product master record
            IF not EOF
                increment product_master_count
            ENDIF
      ENDCASE
END
```

Notice that the three Read instructions in this module perform three separate functions.

Temporal cohesion

Temporal cohesion occurs when the elements of a module are grouped together because they are related by time. Typical examples are initialisation and finalisation modules, where elements are placed together because they perform certain housekeeping functions at the beginning or end of a program.

A temporally cohesive module can be considered a logically cohesive module, where time is the related activity. However, it is slightly stronger than a logically cohesive module because most of the elements in a time related module are executed each time the module is called. Usually, however, the elements are not all related to the same function.

A pseudocode example of a temporally cohesive module might look like this:

```
Initialisation
      Open transaction file
      Issue prompt 'Enter todays date — DDMMYY'
      Read todays_date
      Set transaction_count to zero
      Read transaction record
      IF not EOF
          increment transaction_count
      ENDIF
      Open report file
      Print_page_headings
      Set report_total to zero
END
```

Notice that the elements of the module perform a number of functions.

Procedural cohesion

Procedural cohesion occurs when the elements of a module are related because they operate according to a particular procedure. That is, the elements are executed in a particular sequence so that the objectives of the program are achieved. As a result, the modules contain elements related more to program procedure than to program function.

A typical example of a procedurally cohesive module is the mainline of a program. The elements of a mainline are grouped together because of a particular procedural order.

The weakness of procedurally cohesive modules is that they cut across functional boundaries. That is, the procedure may contain only part of a function at one level, but at the same time may contain multiple functions at a lower level, as in the pseudocode example below:

```
Read_student_records_and_total_student_ages
    Set number_of_records to zero
    Set total_age to zero
    Read student record
    DOWHILE more records exist
        Add age to total_age
        Add 1 to number_of_records
        Read student record
    ENDDO
    Print number_of_records, total_age
END
```

Note that the use of the word 'and' in the module name indicates that this module performs more than one function.

Communicational cohesion

Communicational cohesion occurs when the elements of a module are grouped together because they all operate on the same (central) piece of data. Communicationally cohesive modules are commonly found in business applications because of the close relationship of a business program to the data it is processing. For example, a module may contain all the validations of the fields of a record; or all the processing required to assemble a report line for printing.

Communicational cohesion is acceptable because it is data related. It is stronger than procedural cohesion because of its relationship with the data, rather than the control-flow sequence.

The weakness of a communicationally cohesive module lies in the fact that usually a combination of processing for a particular piece of data is performed, as in this pseudocode example:

```
Validate_product_record
    IF transaction_type NOT = '0' THEN
        error_flag = true
        error_message = 'invalid transaction type'
        Print_error_report
    ENDIF
    IF customer_number is NOT numeric THEN
        error_flag = true
        error_message = 'invalid customer number'
        Print_error_report
    ENDIF
    IF product_no = blanks
    OR product_no has leading blanks THEN
        error_flag = true
        error_message = 'invalid product no'
        Print_error_report
    ENDIF
END
```

Sequential cohesion

Sequential cohesion occurs when a module contains elements which depend on the processing of previous elements. That is, it might contain elements in which the output data from one element serves as input data to the next. Thus, a sequentially cohesive module is like an assembly line: a series of sequential steps perform successive transformations of data.

Sequential cohesion is stronger than communicational cohesion because it is more problem oriented. Its weakness lies only in the fact that the module may perform multiple functions or fragments of functions.

Here is a pseudocode example of a sequentially cohesive module:

```
Process_purchases
    Set total_purchases to zero
    Get number_of_purchases
    DO loop_index = 1 to number_of_purchases
        get purchase
        add purchase to total_purchases
    ENDDO
    sales_tax = total_purchases * sales_tax_percent
    amount_due = total_purchases + sales_tax
END
```

Note that this module first calculates total_purchases and then uses the variable total_purchases in the subsequent calculation of amount_due.

Functional cohesion

Functional cohesion occurs when all the elements of a module contribute to the performance of a single specific task. The module can be easily named by a single verb followed by a two-word object.

Mathematically oriented modules are a good example of functional cohesion, as the elements which make up the module form an integral part of the calculation.

A pseudocode example of a functionally cohesive module is the module Calculate_sales_tax:

```
Calculate_sales_tax
    IF product is sales tax exempt THEN
        sales_tax = 0
    ELSE
        IF product_price < $50.00 THEN
            sales_tax = product_price * 0.25
        ELSE
            IF product_price < $100.00 THEN
                sales_tax = product_price * 0.35
            ELSE
                sales_tax = product_price * 0.5
            ENDIF
        ENDIF
    ENDIF
END
```

Summary of cohesion levels

When designing a program's structure, you should try to form modules which have a single problem-related function. If functional cohesion is achieved, then the modules will be more independent, easier to read and understand, and more maintainable, than modules with lesser cohesion.

In some cases it is not easy to construct a program where every module has functional cohesion. Some modules may contain lower levels of cohesion, or even a combination of types of cohesion. This may not be a problem. However, it is important that you can recognise the various cohesion levels and justify a module with a lower cohesion in a particular set of circumstances.

Your prime consideration is to produce modules and programs which are easy to understand and modify. The higher the cohesion of the modules, the more likely you have achieved this aim.

9.2 MODULE COUPLING

When designing a solution algorithm, look not only at the cohesion of modules but also at the flow of information between modules. You should aim to achieve module independence, i.e. modules which have fewer and simpler connections with other modules. These connections are called interfaces or couples.

Coupling is a measure of the extent of information interchange between modules. Tight coupling implies large dependence on the structure of one module by another. Because there are a higher number of connections, there are many paths along which errors can extend into other parts of the program.

Loose coupling is the opposite of tight coupling. Modules with loose coupling are more independent and easier to maintain.

Glenford Myers[1] devised a coupling scale similar to Yourdon and Constantine's cohesion scale.

Coupling level	Coupling attribute	Resultant module design quality
Common	Tight coupling	poorest
External		
Control	↓	↓
Stamp		
Data	Loose coupling	best

The five levels of coupling are listed in a scale from the poorest module design quality to the best. Each of the levels of coupling will be discussed and pseudocode examples which illustrate each level will be provided. Note that these levels of coupling are not definitive. They are merely those coupling levels which Glenford Myers believes can exist in modular programs.

Common coupling

Common coupling occurs when modules reference the same global data structure. (A data structure is a collection of related data items, such as a record or an array.) When modules experience common coupling, a global data structure is shared by the modules.

This means that the data can be accessed and modified by any module in the program, which can make the program difficult to read.

---

[1] Glenford Myers, *Composite Structured Design*. Van Nostrand Reinhold, 1978.

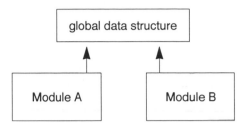

The following pseudocode example shows two modules which experience common coupling because they access the same global data structure (the customer record):

```
A   Read_customer_record
        Read customer record
        IF EOF THEN
            set EOF_flag to true
        ENDIF
    END


B   Validate_customer_record
        IF customer_number is NOT numeric THEN
            error_message = 'invalid customer number'
            Print_error_report
        ENDIF
        :
        :
    END
```

External coupling

External coupling occurs when two or more modules access the same global data variable.

It is similar to common coupling except that the global data is an elementary data item, rather than a data structure. Because the global data has a simpler structure, external coupling is considered to be looser than common coupling.

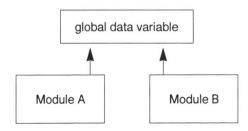

The following pseudocode example shows two modules which exhibit external coupling because they share the same global data item (sales_tax).

```
A   Calculate_sales_tax
        IF product is sales exempt THEN
            sales_tax = 0
        ELSE
            IF product_price < $50.00 THEN
                sales_tax = product_price * 0.25
                    :
                    :
        ENDIF
    END


B   Calculate_amount_due
        :
        :
        amount_due = total_amount + sales_tax
    END
```

Control coupling

Control coupling occurs when a module passes a control variable to another module which is intended to control the other module's logic. These control variables are referred to as program flags, or switches and are passed between modules in the form of parameters.

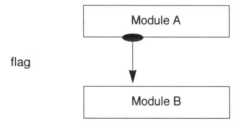

flag

The weakness of control coupled modules is that the passing of the control field between modules implies that one module is aware of the internal logic of the other.

The following pseudocode example shows two modules which are logically cohesive because of the passing of the control parameter (input_code):

```
A   Process_input_code
        Read input_code
        Choose_appropriate_action (input_code)
            :
            :
    END
```

```
B    Choose_appropriate_action (input_code)
          CASE OF input_code
          1 :  Read employee record
          2 :  Print_page_headings
          3 :  Open employee master file
          4 :  Set page_count to zero
          5 :  error_message = 'Employee number not numeric'
          ENDCASE
     END
```

Stamp coupling

Stamp coupling occurs when one module passes a non-global data structure to another module. The non-global data structure is passed in the form of a parameter.

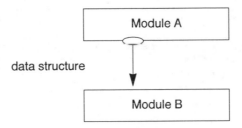

Stamp-coupled modules demonstrate loose coupling and offer good module design quality. The only relationship between the two modules is the passing of the data structure between them; there is no need for either module to know the internal logic of the other.

The following pseudocode example shows two modules which are stamp coupled because of the passing of the data structure current_record.

```
A    Process_transaction_record
          :
          :
          IF transaction record is for a male THEN
               Process_male_student (current_record)
          ELSE
               Process_female_student (current_record)
          ENDIF
          :
          :
     END
```

```
B    Process_male_student (current_record)
         Increment male_student_count
         IF student_age > 21 THEN
             increment mature_male_count
         ENDIF
         :
         :
     END
```

Data coupling

Data coupling occurs when a module passes a non-global data variable to another module. It is similar to stamp coupling except that the non-global data variable is an elementary data item, not a data structure.

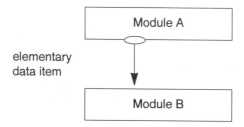

Modules which are data coupled demonstrate the loosest coupling and offer the best module design qualities. The only relationship between the two modules is the passing of one or more elementary data items between them.

The following pseudocode example shows two modules which are data coupled because they pass the elementary data items total_price and sales_tax.

```
A    Process_customer_record
         :
         :
         Calculate_sales_tax (total price, sales_tax)
         :
     END


B    Calculate_sales_tax (total_price, sales_tax)
         IF total_price < $10.00 THEN
             sales_tax = total_price * 0.25
         ELSE
             IF total_price < $100.00 THEN
                 sales_tax = total_price * 0.3
             ELSE
                 sales_tax = total_price * 0.4
             ENDIF
         ENDIF
     END
```

A summary of coupling levels

When designing solution algorithms, you should aim towards module independence and a minimum of information interchange between modules.

If the programming language allows it, try to uncouple each module from its surroundings by:

1   Passing data to a subordinate module in the form of parameters, rather than using global data, and
2   Writing each subordinate module as a self-contained unit which can accept data passed to it; operate on it without reference to other parts of the program; and pass information back to the calling module, if required.

However, your prime consideration must be to produce modules and programs which are easily understood and modified. If the chosen programming language offers only global data, then the fact that the program has been well designed will minimise the effects of tight coupling.

9.3   CHAPTER SUMMARY

This chapter covered a number of different topics which you should consider when designing modular programs. A program which has been well designed has modules which are independent, easy to read and easily maintained. Such modules are likely to exhibit high cohesion and loose coupling.

Cohesion is a measure of the internal strength of a module. The higher the cohesion, the better the module. Seven levels of cohesion were given and each level was discussed, with a pseudocode example provided.

Coupling is a measure of the extent of information interchange between modules. The fewer the connections between modules, the more loosely they are coupled, offering good module design quality. Five levels of coupling were given and each level was discussed, with a pseudocode example provided.

9.4   PROGRAMMING PROBLEMS

As a result of the information on module design in this chapter, you should now look at the solution algorithms which you constructed for all the programming problems given at the end of Chapters 7 and 8. Each solution algorithm should be redesigned so that the modules demonstrate high cohesion and loose coupling. Parameters should be passed between modules to provide greater module independence.

General algorithms for common business problems

A common business problem...

zzz

To provide general pseudocode algorithms to five common business applications. Topics covered are:
—report generation with page break
—single-level control break
—multiple-level control break
—sequential file update
—array processing

OUTLINE

10.1 PROGRAM STRUCTURE

The aim of this chapter is to present a number of general pseudocode solutions to a selection of typical programming problems. All of the features covered in the previous nine chapters have been incorporated into these solutions, with the result that each solution offers a sound modular structure with highly cohesive modules.

For ease of presentation, the solutions have been designed to use global data. They could, however, easily be adjusted to incorporate the passing of parameters as in the examples in Chapter 8.

Throughout this book, reference has been made to a general solution algorithm for the processing of sequential files. This algorithm is a skeleton solution, and in pseudocode looks like this:

```
Process_sequential_file
    Initial processing
    Read first record
    DOWHILE more records exist
        Process this record
        Read next record
    ENDDO
    Final processing
END
```

This basic solution algorithm forms the framework for almost all commercial business programs. It does not include processing for page headings, control breaks, total lines or special calculations. However, you can easily incorporate these requirements by expanding this general solution.

This general solution algorithm can also be modularised:

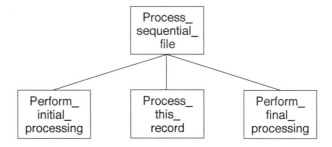

The mainline module would now look like this:

```
Process_sequential_file
    Perform_initial_processing
    Read first record
    DOWHILE more records exist
        Process_this_record
        Read next record
    ENDDO
    Perform_final_processing
END
```

The module Process_this_record can be extended, as required, for the processing of a particular programming problem. We will use this basic program structure to develop solution algorithms to five common business programming applications.

10.2 REPORT GENERATION WITH PAGE BREAK

Most reports require page heading lines, column heading lines, detail lines, and total lines. Reports are also required to skip to a new page after a predetermined number of detail lines have been printed.

A typical report might look like this:

```
                       GLAD RAGS CLOTHING COMPANY
12/05/93                 CURRENT ACCOUNT BALANCES                PAGE: 1
CUSTOMER   CUSTOMER        CUSTOMER                      ACCOUNT
NUMBER     NAME            ADDRESS                       BALANCE
12345      Sporty's Boutique   The Mall, Redfern           300.50
12346      Slinky's Nightwear  245 Picnic Road, Pymble     400.50

                           Total customers on file              200
                           Total customers with balance owning  150
                           Total balance owing              4300.00
```

Our general solution algorithm for processing a sequential file can be extended by the addition of new modules which cater for these report requirements, as follows:

A *Hierarchy chart*

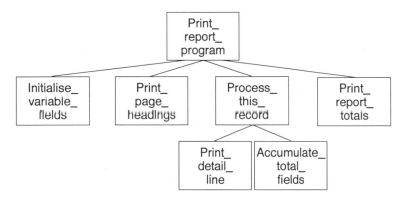

Once the hierarchy chart has been established, the solution algorithm can be developed in pseudocode.

B Solution algorithm

Mainline

```
Print_report_program
    Initialise_variable_fields
    Print_page_headings
    Read first record
    DOWHILE more records exist
        IF line count > max_detail_lines THEN
            Print_page_headings
            set linecount to zero
        ENDIF
        Process_this_record
        Read next record
    ENDDO
    Print_report_totals
END
```

Subordinate modules

```
1   Initialise_variable_fields
        set accumulators to zero
        set pagecount to zero
        set linecount to zero
        set max_detail_lines to designated value
    END
2   Print_page_headings
        increment pagecount
        print heading lines
        print column heading lines
        print blank line (if required)
    END
3   Process_this_record
        Perform necessary calculations (if any)
        Print_detail_line
        Accumulate_total_fields
    END
4   Print_detail_line
        build detail line
        print detail line
        increment linecount
    END
5   Accumulate_total_fields
        increment accumulators as required
    END
6   Print_report_totals
        build total line(s)
        print total line(s)
    END
```

This general pseudocode solution can now be used as a framework for any report program which requires page breaks.

10.3 SINGLE-LEVEL CONTROL BREAK

Printed reports which also produce control break total lines are very common in business applications. A control break total line is a summary line for a group of records which contain the same record key. This record key is a designated field on each record, and is referred to as the control field. The control field is used to identify a record or a group of records within a file. A control break occurs each time there is a change in value of the control field. Thus, control break total lines are printed each time a control break is detected.

Reports which print control break totals can be categorised as being either single-level or multiple-level control break reports depending on whether there is one control field or more than one control field.

Here is a single-level control break report.

	MULTI-DISK COMPUTER COMPANY				
12/05/93	SALES REPORT BY SALESPERSON				PAGE: 1
SALESPERSON NUMBER	SALESPERSON NAME	PRODUCT NUMBER	QTY SOLD	PRICE	EXTENSION AMOUNT
1001	Mary Smith	1032	2	10.00	20.00
		1033	2	20.00	40.00
		1044	2	30.00	60.00
		Sales total for Mary Smith			120.00
1002	Jane Brown	1032	2	10.00	20.00
		1045	1	35.00	35.00
		Sales total for Jane Brown			55.00
		Report sales total			175.00

Note that a control break total line is printed each time the salesperson number changes.

There are two things you must consider when designing a control break program:

1   The file to be processed must have been sorted into control field sequence. (In the example above the file was sorted into ascending sequence of salesperson number.) If the file has not been sorted, erroneous results will occur.

2   Each time a record is read from the input file, the control field on the current record must be compared with the control field on the previous

record just printed. If the control fields are different a control break total line must be printed for the previous set of records, i.e. before the current record is processed.

The general solution algorithm which was developed for a Report Generation program can be extended by the addition of two new modules to incorporate a single-level control break. These modules are named Print_control_total_line and Reset_control_totals.

A *Hierarchy chart*

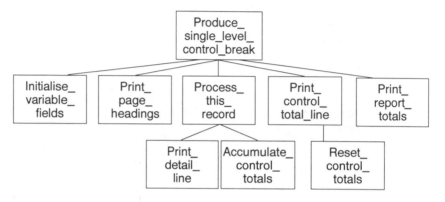

All control break report programs will require the following variables:

1   A variable named this_control_field which will hold the control field of the record just read.
2   A variable named prev_control_field which will hold the control field of the previous record. (To cater for the first record, the statements after the first Read statement will set the new control field to both the variable this_control_field and prev_control_field.)
3   One or more variables to accumulate the control break totals.
4   A variable to accumulate the report totals.

B *Solution algorithm*
Mainline

```
Produce_single_level_control_break
        Initialise_variable_fields
        Print_page_headings
        Read first record
        this_control_field = control field
        prev_control_field = control field
        DOWHILE more records exist
```

```
              IF this_control_field NOT = prev_control_field THEN
                  Print_control_total_line
                  prev_control_field = this_control_field
              ENDIF
              IF linecount > max_detail_lines THEN
                  Print_page_headings
                  set linecount to zero
              ENDIF
              Process_this_record
              Read next record
              this_control_field = control field
          ENDDO
          Print_control_total_line
          Print_report_totals
      END
```

There are four points in this mainline algorithm which are essential for a control break program to function correctly:

1   Each time a new record is read from the file, the new control field is assigned to the variable this_control_field.
2   When the first record is read, the new control field is assigned to both the variables this_control_field and prev_control_field. This will prevent the control totals printing before the first record has been processed.
3   The variable prev_control_field is updated as soon as a change in the control field is detected.
4   After the end of the file has been detected, the module Print_control_total_line is called. This will then print the control break totals for the last record or set of records.

Subordinate modules

```
      1   Initialise_variable_fields
              set control total accumulators to zero
              set report total accumulators to zero
              set pagecount to zero
              set linecount to zero
              set max_detail_lines to designated value
          END
      2   Print_page_headings
              increment pagecount
              print heading lines
              print column heading lines
              print blank line (if required)
          END
```

```
3   Process_this_record
        Perform necessary calculations (if any)
        Print_detail_line
        Accumulate_control_totals
    END
4   Print_control_total_line
        build control total line
        print control total line
        print blank line (if required)
        increment linecount
        Reset_control_totals
    END
5   Print_report_totals
        build report total line
        print report total line
    END
6   Print_detail_line
        build detail line
        print detail line
        increment linecount
    END
7   Accumulate_control_totals
        increment control total accumulators
    END
8   Reset_control_totals
        add control total accumulators to report total accumulators
        set control total accumulators to zero
    END
```

Notice that when a control total line is printed, the module Reset_control_totals is called. This module will add the control totals to the report totals and reset the control totals to zero for the next set of records. This general solution algorithm can now be used as a framework for any single-level control break program.

10.4   MULTIPLE-LEVEL CONTROL BREAK

Often reports are required to produce multiple-level control break totals. For instance, the Sales Report produced in section 10.3 may require sales totals for each salesperson in the company as well as sales totals for each department within the company.

The Monthly Sales Report might then look like this:

MULTI-DISK COMPUTER COMPANY

12/05/93		SALES REPORT BY SALESPERSON				PAGE: 1
DEPT	SALESPERSON NUMBER	SALESPERSON NAME	PRODUCT NUMBER	QTY SOLD	PRICE	EXTENSION AMOUNT
01	1001	Mary Smith	1032	2	10.00	20.00
			1033	2	20.00	40.00
			1044	2	30.00	60.00
			Sales total for Mary Smith			120.00
	1002	Jane Brown	1032	2	10.00	20.00
			1045	1	35.00	35.00
			Sales total for Jane Brown			55.00
			Sales total for Dept 01			175.00
02	1050	Jenny Ponds	1033	2	20.00	40.00
			1044	2	30.00	60.00
			Sales total for Jenny Ponds			100.00
			Sales total for Dept 02			100.00
			Report sales total			275.00

Note that a control break total line is printed each time the salesperson number changes, and each time the department number changes. Thus, there are two control fields in this file.

The concepts which applied to a single-level control break program also apply to a multiple-level control break program:

1   The input file must be sorted into control field sequence. When there is more than one control field, the file must be sorted into a sequence of minor control field within major control field. (To produce the Sales Report, the Sales File must have been sorted into salesperson number within department number.)

2   Each time a record is read from the file, the control fields on the current record must be compared with the control fields of the record just printed. If the minor control fields have changed, then the control totals for the previous minor control field must be printed. If the major control fields have changed, then the control fields for the previous major control field and minor control field must be printed.

The general solution algorithm which was developed for a single-level control break program can be extended by the addition of two new modules to incorporate a two-level control break. If three control breaks were required, then another two modules would be added to the solution algorithm, and so on.

The names of the modules which produce the control totals have been changed slightly, so that they indicate which level of control break has occurred.   These new module names are: Print_minor_control_totals, Print_major_control_totals, Reset_minor_control_totals, and Reset_major_ control_totals.

A Hierarchy chart

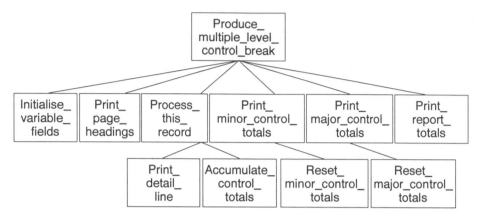

B Solution algorithm

Mainline

```
Produce_multiple_level_control_break
        Initialise_variable_fields
        Print_page_headings
        Read first record
        this_minor_control_field = minor control field
        prev_minor_control_field = minor control field
        this_major_control_field = major control field
        prev_major_control_field = major control field
        DOWHILE more records exist
            IF this_major_control_field NOT = prev_major_control_field THEN
                Print_minor_control_totals
                prev_minor_control_field = this_minor_control_field
                Print_major_control_totals
                prev_major_control_field = this_major_control_field
            ELSE
                IF this_minor_control_field NOT = prev_minor_control_field THEN
                    Print_minor_control_totals
                    prev_minor_control_field = this_minor_control_field
                ENDIF
            ENDIF
            IF linecount > max_detail_lines THEN
                Print_page_headings
                set linecount to zero
```

```
            ENDIF
            Process_this_record
            Read next record
            this_minor_control_field = minor control field
            this_major_control_field = major control field
        ENDDO
        Print_minor_control_totals
        Print_major_control_totals
        Print_report_totals
    END
```

The points to be noted in this mainline are:

1   Each time a new record is read from the input file, the new control fields are assigned to the variables this_minor control_field and this_major_control_field.
2   When the first record is read, the new control fields are assigned to both the current and previous control field variables. This will prevent control totals printing before the first record has been processed.
3   After the end of the input file has been detected, the two modules Print_minor_control_totals and Print_major_control_totals will be called. This will then print control totals for the last minor control field record, or set of records, and the last major control field set of records.

Subordinate modules

```
    1   Initialise_variable_fields
            set minor control total accumulators to zero
            set major control total accumulators to zero
            set report total accumulators to zero
            set pagecount to zero
            set linecount to zero
            set max_detail_lines to designated value
        END
    2   Print_page_headings
            increment page counter
            print heading lines
            print column heading lines
            print blank line (if required)
        END
    3   Process_this_record
            Perform necessary calculations (if any)
            Print_detail_line
            Accumulate_control_totals
        END
```

```
4    Print_minor_control_totals
          build minor control total line
          print minor control total line
          print blank line (if required)
          increment linecount
          Reset_minor_control_totals
     END
5    Print_major_control_totals
          build major control total line
          print major control total line
          print blank line (if required)
          increment linecount
          Reset_major_control_totals
     END
6    Print_report_totals
          build report total line
          print report total line
     END
7    Print_detail_line
          build detail line
          print detail line
          increment linecount
     END
8    Accumulate_control_totals
          increment minor control total accumulators
     END
9    Reset_minor_control_totals
          add minor control total accumulators to major control total accumulators
          set minor control total accumulators to zero
     END
10   Reset_major_control_totals
          add major control total accumulators to report total accumulators
          set major control total accumulators to zero
     END
```

Because the solution algorithm has simple design, and good modular structure, the processing of intermediate control field breaks as well as major and minor control field breaks can be handled easily. The solution algorithm would simply require the addition of two new modules: Print_intrmed_control_totals and Reset_intrmed_control_totals. The IF statement in the mainline would then be expanded to include this extra condition, as follows:

```
IF this_major_control_field NOT = prev_major_control_field THEN
    Print_minor_control_totals
    prev_minor_control_field = this_minor_control_field
    Print_intrmed_control_totals
    prev_intrmed_control_field = this_intrmed_control_field
    Print_major_control_totals
    prev_major_control_field = this_major_control_field
ELSE
    IF this_intrmed_control_field NOT = prev_intrmed_control_field THEN
        Print_minor_control_totals
        prev_minor_control_field = this_minor_control_field
        Print_intrmed_control_totals
        prev_intrmed_control_field = this_intrmed_control_field
    ELSE
        IF this_minor_control_field NOT = prev_minor_control_field THEN
            Print_minor_control_totals
            prev_minor_control_field = this_minor_control_field
        ENDIF
    ENDIF
ENDIF
```

This pseudocode algorithm can now be used to process any multiple-level control break program.

10.5 SEQUENTIAL FILE UPDATE

Sequential file updating is a very common batch processing application. It involves updating a master file by the application of update transactions on a transaction file. Both files are sequential. A new master file which incorporates the update transactions is produced. Usually, audit reports and error reports are also printed.

A system flow chart of a sequential update program would look like this:

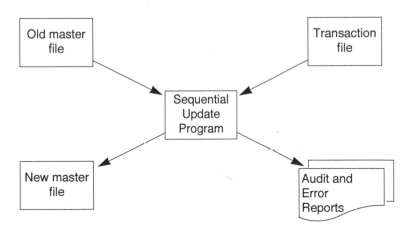

System concepts

1   Master file

A master file is a file which contains permanent and semi-permanent information about the data entities it contains. The records on the master file are in sequence, according to a key field (or fields) on each record. For example, a customer master file may contain the customer's name, address, phone number, credit rating and current balance.

2   Transaction file

A transaction file contains all the data and activities which are included on the master file. If the transaction file has been designed specifically to update a master file, then there are usually three types of update transactions on this file. These are transactions to:

- add a new record,
- update or change an existing record, and
- delete an existing record.

For example, a customer transaction file might contain transactions which are intended to add a new customer record, change some data on an existing customer record, or delete a customer record on the customer master file. The transaction file is also in sequence according to the same key field as the master record.

3   Audit report

An audit report is a detailed list of all the transactions which were applied to the master file. It provides an accounting trail of the update activities which take place, and is used for control purposes.

4   Error report

An error report is a detailed list of errors which occurred during the processing of the update. Typical errors might be the attempted update of a record which is not on the master file, or the addition of a record which already exists. This error report will require some action to confirm and correct the identified errors.

Sequential update logic

The logic of a sequential update program is more difficult than the other problems encountered, because there are two sequential input files.

Processing involves reading a record from each of the input files and comparing the keys of the two records. As a result of this comparison, processing falls generally into three categories:

1   If the transaction record key is less than the old master record key, the transaction is probably an add transaction. The details on the transaction record should be put into master record format, and the record should be written to the new master file. Another record should then be read from the transaction file.
2   If the transaction record key is equal to the old master record key, then the transaction is probably an update or delete transaction. If the transaction is an update, the master record should be amended to reflect the required changes. If the transaction is a delete, the master record should not be written to the new master file. Another transaction record should then be read from the transaction file.
3   If the transaction record key is greater than the old master record key, there is no matching transaction for that master record. In this case the old master record should be written unchanged to the new master file and another record read from the old master file.

Sequential update programs also need to include logic which will handle multiple transaction records for the same master record, and the possibility of transaction records which are in error. The types of transaction record errors which can occur are:

1   An attempt to add a new master record when a record with that key already exists on the master file.
2   An attempt to update a master record when there is no record with that key on the master file.
3   An attempt to delete a master record when there is no record with that key on the master file.
4   An attempt to delete a master record when the current balance is not equal to zero.

Balance line algorithm

The logic of the sequential update program has fascinated programmers for many years. Authors have offered many solutions to the problem, but none of these have been a truly general solution. Most solutions have been designed around a specific programming language.

A good general solution algorithm written in pseudocode was presented by Barry Dwyer in a paper entitled 'One More Time — How to Update a Master File'[1]. This algorithm has been referred to as the balance line algorithm. It handles multiple transaction records for the one master record as well as the possibility of transaction record errors.

A modularised version of the balance line algorithm is presented in this chapter. It introduces the concept of a current record. The current record is the record which is currently being processed, ready for updating and writing to the new master file. The current record is established when the record keys on the two files are compared. The current record will be the record which has the smaller record key. Its format will be that of a new master record.

Thus, if the transaction record key is less than the old master key, the current record will be made up of the fields on the transaction record. If the transaction record key is equal to or greater than the old master record key, the old master record will become the current record.

The current record will remain the current record until there are no more transactions to be applied to that record. It will then be written to the new master file, and a new current record will be established.

Another variable, current_record_status, is used as a program flag to indicate whether or not the current record is available for processing. If the current_record_status is active, then the current record has been established and is available for updating or writing out to the new master file. If the current_record_status is inactive, then the current record is not available to be updated or written to the new master file, e.g. the current record may have been marked for deletion.

The processing of the two files will continue until end_of_job has been reached. End_of_job will occur when both the input files have no more data to be processed. Since it is not known which file will reach end of file (EOF) first, the record key of each file will be set to a high value when EOF is reached. When the record key of one of the files is high, the other file will continue to be processed, as required, until the record key on that file is assigned the same high value. End_of_job occurs when the record keys on both the files is the same high value.

Let us now establish a general solution algorithm for a sequential update program. The logic provided will also include the printing of the audit and error reports.

[1] Barry Dwyer, 'One More Time — How to Update a Master File'. *Comm. ACM*, Vol. 124, No. 1, January 1981.

A   Hierarchy chart

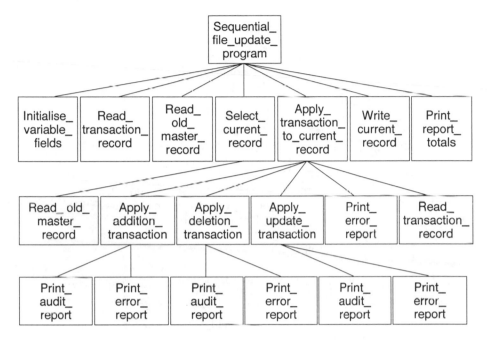

B   Solution algorithm

Mainline

```
Sequential_update_program
    Initialise_variable_fields
    Read_transaction_record
    Read_old_master_record
    set current_record_status to 'inactive'
    DOWHILE NOT end_of_job
        Select_current_record
        DOWHILE transaction_record_key = current_record_key
            Apply_transaction_to_current_record
        ENDDO
        IF current_record_status = 'active' THEN
            Write_current_record
            set current_record_status to 'inactive'
        ENDIF
    ENDDO
    Print_report_totals
END
```

Subordinate modules

1   Initialise_variable_fields
        set total_transaction_records to zero
        set total_old_master_records to zero
        set total_new_master_records to zero
        set total_error_records to zero
        set end_of_job to false
    END
2   Read_transaction_record
        Read transaction record
        IF NOT EOF THEN
            increment total_transaction_records
        ELSE
            set transaction_record_key to high value
            IF old_master_record_key = high value THEN
                set end_of_job to true
            ENDIF
        ENDIF
    END
3   Read_old_master_record
        Read old master record
        IF NOT EOF THEN
            increment total_old_master_records
        ELSE
            set old_master_record_key to high value
            IF transaction_record_key = high value THEN
                set end_of_job = true
            ENDIF
        ENDIF
    END
4   Select_current_record
        IF transaction_record_key < old_master_record_key THEN
            set up current record with transaction record fields
        ELSE
            set up current record with old master record fields
            set current_record_status to 'active'
            Read_old_master_record
        ENDIF
    END
5   Apply_transaction_to_current_record
        CASE OF transaction_type
            addition : Apply_addition_transaction
            deletion : Apply_deletion_transaction
            update : Apply_update_transaction
            other : error_message = 'invalid transaction type'
                    Print_error_report
        ENDCASE
        Read_transaction_record
    END

6   Write_current_record
          write current record to new master file
          increment total_new_master_records
    END
7   Print_report_totals
          print total_transaction_records
          print total_old_master_records
          print total_new_master_records
          print total_error_records
    END
8   Apply_addition_transaction
          IF current_record_status = 'inactive' THEN
             set current_record_status to 'active'
             Print_audit_report
          ELSE
             error_message = 'Invalid addition; record already exists'
             Print_error_report
          ENDIF
    END
9   Apply_deletion_transaction
          IF current_record_status = 'active' THEN
             set current_record_status to 'inactive'
             Print_audit_report
          ELSE
             error_message = 'Invalid deletion, record not on master file'
             Print_error_report
          ENDIF
    END
10   Apply_update_transaction
          IF current_record_status = 'active' THEN
             apply required change(s) to current record
             Print_audit_report
          ELSE
             error_message = 'Invalid update; record not on master file'
             Print_error_report
          ENDIF
    END
11   Print_audit_report
          print transaction details on audit report
          CASE OF transaction_type
             addition : print 'record added'
             deletion : print 'record deleted'
             update : print 'record updated'
          ENDCASE
    END
12   Print_error_report
          print transaction details on error report
          print error_message
          increment total_error_records
    END

Note that end_of_job is reached when the transaction_record_key = high value AND the old_master_record_key = high value. This pseudocode algorithm can now be used to process any sequential file update report.

10.6 ARRAY PROCESSING

An array is a data structure, which is made up of a number of variables which all have the same data type; for example, all the exam scores for a class.

The individual data items which make up the array are referred to as the elements of the array. They are assigned a single data name, e.g. scores (the name of the array). The individual elements of an array can be distinguished from each other by a subscript or index. The subscript indicates the position of the element within the array; e.g. scores(3) points to the third element in the array scores.

Arrays are an internal data structure, i.e. they are required only for the duration of the program in which they are defined. They are a very convenient mechanism for storing and manipulating a collection of similar data items in a program, and you should be familiar with the operations most commonly performed on them.

This section will develop pseudocode algorithms for the most typical operations performed on arrays:

- reading values into the elements of an array,
- a linear search of an array,
- a binary search of an array, and
- writing out the contents of an array.

Reading values into the elements of an array

The reading of a series of values from a file into an array can be represented by a simple DOWHILE loop. The loop should terminate when either the array is full or the input file has reached end of file.

Both these conditions can be catered for in the condition clause of the DOWHILE loop. In the following pseudocode algorithm, the array name is array, the subscript index, and the value being put into the element of the array is input value. The maximum number of elements which the array can hold is placed in max_num_elements.

```
Read_values_into_array
    set max_num_elements to designated value
    set index to zero
    read first input value
    DOWHILE (input values exist AND index < max_num_elements)
```

```
            index = index + 1
            array (index) = input value
            read next input value
        ENDDO
    END
```

A linear search of an array

A common operation on arrays is to search the elements of an array for a particular data item. A linear search involves looking at each of the elements of the array, one by one, starting with the first element. The search will continue until the element being looked for is found or the end of the array is reached.

The pseudocode algorithm for a linear search of an array will require a program flag named element_found. This flag, initially set to false, will be set to true if the current element is the data item being looked for. The required data item is stored in the variable input_value, and max_num_elements contains the total number of elements in the array.

```
Linear_search_of_an_array
    set max_num_elements to designated value
    set element_found to false
    set index to 1
    DOWHILE (NOT element_found AND index ≤ max_num_elements)
        IF array (index) = input value THEN
            set element_found to true
        ELSE
            index = index + 1
        ENDIF
    ENDDO
END
```

A binary search of an array

When the number of elements in an array exceeds 25 and the elements are sorted into ascending sequence, a more efficient method of searching the array is a binary search.

A binary search locates the middle element of the array first, and determines if the element being searched for is in the first half or second half of the table. The search then points to the middle element of the relevant half table, and the comparison is then repeated. This technique of continually halving the area under consideration is continued until the data item being searched for is found or its absence is detected.

In the following algorithm, a program flag named element_found is used to indicate whether the data item being looked for has been found. The variable low_element indicates the bottom position of the section of the table being searched, and high_element indicates the top position. The maximum number of elements which the array can hold is placed in the variable max_num_elements.

The binary search will continue until the data item has been found or there can be no more halving operations (i.e. low_element is not less than high_element).

```
Binary_search_of_an_array
    set element_found to false
    set low_element to 1
    set high_element to max_num_elements
    DOWHILE (NOT element_found AND low_element ≤ high_element)
        index = (low_element + high_element) / 2
        IF input value = array(index) THEN
            set element_found to true
        ELSE
            IF input value < array(index) THEN
                high_element = index − 1
            ELSE
                low_element = index + 1
            ENDIF
        ENDIF
    ENDDO
END
```

Writing out the contents of an array

The elements of arrays are often used as a series of accumulators of data, to be written to a report. Writing out the contents of an array can be represented by a simple DOWHILE loop.

In the pseudocode algorithm, the name of the array is array and the subscript is index. The number of elements in the array is represented by max_num_elements.

```
Write_values_of_array
    set index to 1
    DOWHILE index ≤ max_num_elements
        write array(index)
        index = index + 1
    ENDDO
END
```

10.7 CHAPTER SUMMARY

The aim of this chapter was to develop general pseudocode algorithms to five common business applications. The applications covered were:

- report generation with page break,
- single-level control break,
- multiple-level control break,
- sequential file update, and
- array processing.

In each section, the application was discussed, a hierarchy chart was developed, and a general solution algorithm was presented in pseudocode. These solution algorithms can be used when writing programs which incorporate any of the above applications.

10.8 PROGRAMMING PROBLEMS

Design a solution algorithm for the following programming problems. Your solution should contain:

- a defining diagram,
- a hierarchy chart,
- a pseudocode algorithm, and
- a desk check of the solution.

1   Design a program to read the Customer Master File of a clothing manufacturer, and print a report of all the customer records which have an account balance greater than zero.

The Customer Master File contains the customer number, name, address (street, city, state and postcode), and the customer's account balance.

The output report must show all the customers' details and three total lines as indicated. There are to be 35 detail lines per page.

		GLAD RAGS CLOTHING COMPANY	
XX/XX/XX		CURRENT ACCOUNTS BALANCES	PAGE· XX
CUSTOMER NUMBER	CUSTOMER NAME	ADDRESS	ACCOUNT BALANCE
XXXXX	XXXXXXXXXX	XXXXXXXXXXXXXXXXXXX	9 999.99
XXXXX	XXXXXXXXXX	XXXXXXXXXXXXXXXXXXX	9 999.99
:	:	:	:
		Total customers on file	999
		Total customers with balance owing	999
		Total balance owing	99 999.99

2   Design a program which will read the Sales File for the Multi-Disk
Computer Company, and produce a Sales Report according to
salesperson. The Sales Report shows the details of each sale made per
salesperson, and a total of the sales for that salesperson.

The fields on the Sales File are the salesperson's number and name,
the product number of the product sold, the quantity sold and the price
of the product. There may be many records for each salesperson,
depending on the products sold that month. The Sales File has been
sorted into ascending sequence of salesperson number.

Your program is to read the Sales File sequentially, calculate the
extension amount (price * quantity sold) for each product sold and print
a detail line for each record processed. Control total lines showing the
sales total for each salesperson are to be printed on change of
salesperson number.

The report details are to be printed, as per the following Sales
Report:

MULTI-DISK COMPUTER COMPANY

XX/XX/XX	SALES REPORT BY SALESPERSON				PAGE: XX
SALESPERSON NUMBER	SALESPERSON NAME	PRODUCT NUMBER	QTY SOLD	PRICE	EXTENSION AMOUNT
xxxx	xxxxxxxxxx	xxxx	99	999.99	9 999.99
		xxxx	99	999.99	9 999.99
		xxxx	99	999.99	9 999.99
		Sales total for xxxxxxxxxx			99 999.99
		Report sales total			999 999.99

3   The same Sales File as described in Problem 2 exists, with the addition
of a further field, department number. The Sales File has been sorted
into ascending sequence of salesperson number within department
number. The same Sales Report is to be printed, with the additional
requirement of a sales total on change of department number, as well as
salesperson number.

The report details are to be printed as per the following Sales Report:

MULTI-DISK COMPUTER COMPANY

XX/XX/XX		SALES REPORT				PAGE: XX
DEPT	SALESPERSON NUMBER	SALESPERSON NAME	PRODUCT NUMBER	QTY SOLD	PRICE	EXTENSION AMOUNT
xx	xxxx	xxxxxxxxxx	xxxx	99	999.99	9 999.99
			xxxx	99	999.99	9 999.99
			xxxx	99	999.99	9 999.99
			Sales total for xxxxxxxxxx			99 999.99
			Sales total for Dept xx			999 999.99
			Report sales total			9999 999.99

4 The Yummy Chocolates Confectionery Company requires a program to sequentially update its Customer Master File. A sequential file of update transactions is to be used as the input file, along with the Customer Master file.

The Customer Master File contains the customer number, customer name, customer address (street, city, state and postcode) and account balance. The Customer Transaction File contains the same fields, as well as a transaction code of 'A' (add), 'D' (delete) and 'U' (update).

Both files have been sorted into customer number sequence. There can be multiple update transactions for any one Customer Master record, and a new Customer Master File is to be created.

Transaction records are to be processed as follows:

1 If the transaction record is an Add, the transaction is to be written to the New Customer Master File.

2 If the transaction record is a Delete, the Old Master record with the same customer number is not to be written to the New Customer Master File.

3 If the transaction record is an Update, the Old Master record with the same customer number is to be updated as follows:

- if customer name is present, update customer name;
- if street is present, update street;
- if town is present, update town;
- if state is present, update state;
- if postcode is present, update postcode; and
- if balance paid is present, subtract balance paid from account balance on old customer master record.

As each transaction is processed, the transaction details are to be printed on the Customer Master Audit Report with the message, 'record added', 'record deleted' or 'record updated' as applicable.

If a transaction record is in error, the transaction details are to be printed on the Customer Update Errors Report, with one of the following messages:

- 'invalid addition, customer already exists'
- 'invalid deletion, customer not on file'
- 'invalid update, customer not on file'.

5   A program is required to validate the product code on a Product Transaction File. A file of valid product codes is to be read into an array at the beginning of the program. There can be up to 300 products at any time.

Once the product codes have been set up in the array, the Product Transaction file is to be read sequentially. The product code on each transaction record is to be validated by searching the array for that product code. If the search is successful, then no further action is to take place. If the product code is not found in the array, then the transaction record is to be written to the Transaction Errors Report, with the message 'invalid transaction code'. Totals at the end of the report should include the total number of valid and invalid transactions.

Conclusion

OBJECTIVES

▨   Revision of the steps required to achieve good program design

OUTLINE

11.1 Simple program design
11.2 Chapter summary

11.1   SIMPLE PROGRAM DESIGN

The aim of this textbook has been to encourage programmers to follow a series of simple steps in order to develop solution algorithms to given programming problems. These steps are:

1   Define the problem. To do this, underline the nouns and verbs in the problem description. This helps to divide the problem into its input, output and processing components. These components can be represented in a defining diagram — a table which lists the inputs to the problem, the expected outputs, and the processing steps required to produce these outputs.

     At this stage you should be concerned only with what needs to be done. So when writing down the processing components, you should simply list the activities to be performed without being concerned about how to perform them.

2   Group the activities into subtasks or functions. To do this, look at the defining diagram and group the activities in the processing component into separate tasks. There are often several activities listed in the processing component which all contribute to the performance of a single task. These separate tasks are called functions. By grouping the activities together to form subtasks, you are establishing the major functions of the problem.

     Not all the activities to be performed may have been listed in the defining diagram. If the problem is large, only the top-level subtasks may have been identified at this stage. The basic aim of top-down design is to develop the higher-level modules first, and to develop the lower-level modules only when the higher-level modules have been established. You should concentrate on these higher-level functions before attempting to consider further subordinate functions.

3   Construct a hierarchy chart. To do this, study the defining diagram, which now has the major tasks identified on it, and illustrate these tasks or functions on a hierarchy chart. The functions identified on the hierarchy chart will become the future modules of the program.

     The hierarchy chart shows not only the modules of the program, but also their relationship to each other, in a similar fashion to the organisational chart of a large company.

     Just as a company director can change the organisation of the company to suit its operation, so you can change the organisation of the modules in the hierarchy chart. It is good programming practice to study the way the modules have been organised in the overall structure of the program, and to attempt to make this structure as simple and top-down as possible.

Note that you are still only concerned with what tasks are to be performed. Once the hierarchical structure of the algorithm has been developed, you can begin to consider the logic of the solution.

4   Establish the logic of the mainline of the algorithm. You can use pseudocode and the three basic control structures to establish this logic. Pseudocode is a subset of English which has been formalised and abbreviated to look like a high-level computer language. Keywords and indentation are used to signify particular control structures. The three basic control structures are simple sequence, selection and repetition.

Because you will have already identified the major functions of the problem, you can now use pseudocode and the three control structures to develop the mainline logic. This mainline should show the main processing functions of the problem and the order in which they are to be performed.

We saw that the mainline for most algorithms follows the same basic pattern. This pattern contains some initial processing before the loop, some processing of the record within the loop, and some final processing after exiting the loop.

Chapter 10 developed a general pseudocode algorithm for five common business applications. These algorithms were for the generation of a report with a page break, a single-level control break program, a multiple-level control break program, a sequential file update program and some algorithms used in the processing of arrays. The algorithms which were developed have good program structure and high modular cohesion, and you should use these algorithms as a guide for specific programming problems.

5   Develop the pseudocode for each successive module in the hierarchy chart. The algorithms for these modules should be developed in a top-down fashion. That is, the pseudocode for each module on the first level should be established, before attempting the pseudocode for the modules on the next or lower level. The modularisation process is complete when the pseudocode for each module on the lowest level of the hierarchy chart has been developed.

6   Desk check the solution algorithm. By desk checking the algorithm, you attempt to find any logic errors which have crept into the solution.

Desk checking involves tracing through the logic of the algorithm with some chosen test data exactly as the computer would operate. The programmer keeps track of all major variables in a table as he or she walks through the algorithm. At the end of the desk check, the programmer checks that the output expected from the test data matches the output developed in the desk check.

This detection of errors, early in the design process, can save many frustrating hours during the testing phase. This is because when the programmer begins coding, he or she assumes that the logic of the algorithm is correct. Then, when errors occur, the programmer usually concentrates on the individual lines of code, rather than the initial logic expressed in the algorithm.

It is essential that the programmer desk checks the solution algorithm, and yet this step is so often ignored. Most programmers who bypass this step do so because they either assume the algorithm is correct, or because they believe desk checking is not creative. While it may not be as stimulating as the original design phase, it is really just as satisfying to know that the logic is correct.

11.2   CHAPTER SUMMARY

This chapter has revised the steps required to achieve good program design. Program design is considered good if it is easy to read and understand and easy to alter.

If you follow these six steps in the development of an algorithm, you will rapidly achieve a high level of competence.

Nassi-Schneiderman diagrams

Nassi-Schneiderman (N-S) diagrams are very similar to pseudocode. They simply offer a more diagrammatic approach for those who prefer a visual method of representation. In this appendix the three basic control structures as set out in the Structure Theorem will be explained and illustrated using Nassi-Schneiderman diagrams.

THE THREE BASIC CONTROL STRUCTURES

1   Sequence

The sequence control structure is the straightforward execution of one processing step after another. An N-S diagram represents this control structure as a series of rectangular boxes, one beneath the other:

| statement a |
| statement b |
| statement c |

The sequence control structure can be used to represent the first four basic computer operations: receive information, put out information, perform arithmetic, and assign values. For example a typical sequence of statements in an N-S diagram might read:

| Add 1 to page_count |
| Write heading line |
| Set linecount to zero |
| Read customer record |

These instructions illustrate the sequence control structure as a straightforward list of steps, written one after the other, in a top-to-bottom fashion. Each instruction will be executed in the order in which it appears.

2   Selection

The selection control structure is the presentation of a condition, and the choice between two actions depending on whether the condition is true or false. This construct represents the decision-making abilities of the computer and is used to illustrate the fifth basic computer operation, namely to compare two pieces of information and select one of two alternative actions. An N-S diagram represents the selection control structure pictorially as the testing of a condition which can lead to two separate paths:

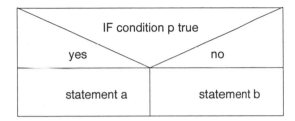

If condition p is true, the statement or statements in the yes box will be executed. If condition p is false, the statement or statements in the no box will be executed. Both paths then lead to the next box following the selection control structure. A typical N-S diagram might look like this:

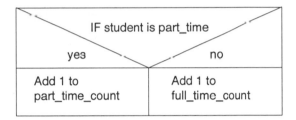

A variation of the selection control structure is the null ELSE structure, which is used when a task is performed only if a particular condition is true. The N-S diagram which represents the null ELSE construct simply leaves the 'no' box blank, or includes the words 'no action' in that box.

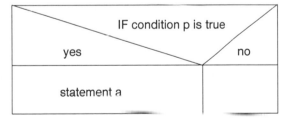

3   Repetition

The repetition control structure can be defined as the presentation of a set of instructions to be performed repeatedly, as long as a condition is true. The basic idea of repetitive code is that a block of statements is executed again and again, until a terminating condition occurs. This construct represents the sixth basic computer operation, namely to repeat a group of actions. An N-S diagram represents this structure as one rectangular box inside an L-shaped frame:

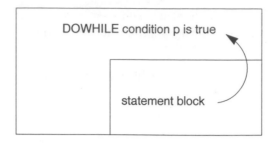

While condition p is true, the statements inside the rectangular box will be executed. The last line of the box acts as the delimiter, and returns control to retest condition p (see up arrow). When condition p is false, control will pass out of the repetition structure down the false path to the next statement (see down arrow).

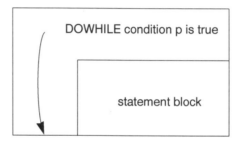

This N-S diagram represents the repetition control structure:

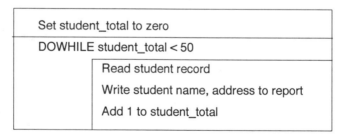

SIMPLE ALGORITHMS WHICH USE THE SEQUENCE CONTROL STRUCTURE

The following examples are the same as those represented by pseudocode in Chapter 3. In each example, the problem is defined and a solution algorithm developed using a Nassi-Schneiderman diagram. To help define the problem, the processing verbs in each example have been underlined.

EXAMPLE 3.1 *Add three numbers*

A program is required to <u>read</u> three numbers, <u>add</u> them <u>together</u> and <u>print</u> their total.

A Defining diagram

Input	Processing	Output
number_1	Read three numbers	total
number_2	Add numbers together	
number_3	Print total number	

(B) Solution algorithm

Add_three_numbers

Read number_1, number_2, number_3
total = number_1 + number_2 + number_3
Print total

EXAMPLE 3.2 *Find average temperature*

A program is required to <u>prompt</u> the terminal operator for the maximum and minimum temperature readings on a particular day, <u>accept</u> those readings as integers, and <u>calculate</u> and <u>display</u> to the screen the simple average temperature [(maximum + minimum / 2)].

A Defining diagram

Input	Processing	Output
max_temp	Prompt for temperatures	avg_temp
min_temp	Get max, min temperatures	
	Calculate average temperature	
	Display average temperature	

B Solution algorithm

Find_average_temperature

Prompt operator for max_temp, min_temp
Get max_temp, min_temp
avg_temp = (max_temp + min_temp) / 2
Output avg_temp to the screen

EXAMPLE 3.3 *Calculate mowing time*

A program is required to <u>read</u> in the length and width of a rectangular house block, and the length and width of the rectangular house which has been built on the block. The algorithm should then <u>compute</u> and <u>display</u> the time required to cut the grass around the house, at the rate of two square metres per minute.

A *Defining diagram*

Input	Processing	Output
block_length	Prompt for block measurements	mowing_time
block_width	Get block measurements	
house_length	Prompt for house measurements	
house_width	Get house measurements	
	Calculate mowing area	
	Calculate mowing time	

B *Solution algorithm*

Calculate_mowing_time

Prompt operator for block_length, block_width
Get block_length, block_width
block_area = block_length * block_width
Prompt operator for house_length, house_width
Get house_length, house_width
house_area = house_length * house_width
mowing_area = block_area – house_area
mowing_time = mowing_area / 2
Output mowing_time to screen

N-S DIAGRAMS AND THE SELECTION CONTROL STRUCTURE

Each variation of the selection control structure developed with pseudocode in Chapter 4 can similarly be represented using a Nassi-Schneiderman diagram.

Simple IF statement

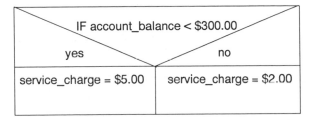

Null ELSE statement

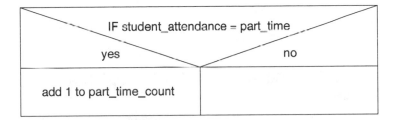

Combined IF statement

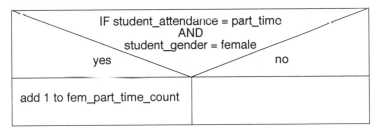

Nested IF statement

A *Linear nested IF statement*

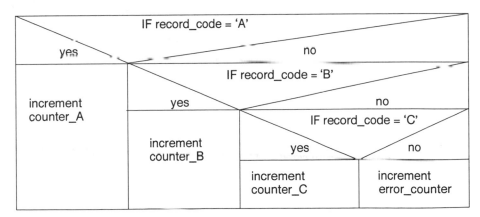

B Non-linear nested IF statement

IF student_attendance = part_time			
yes			no
IF student_gender = female			add 1 to full_time_students
yes		no	
IF student_age > 21		add 1 to male_pt_students	
yes	no		
add 1 to mature_fem_ pt_students	add 1 to young_fem_ pt_students		

SIMPLE ALGORITHMS WHICH USE THE SELECTION CONTROL STRUCTURE

The following examples are the same as those represented by pseudocode in Chapter 4. In each example, the problem is defined and a solution algorithm developed using a Nassi-Schneiderman diagram. The processing verbs in each example have been underlined.

EXAMPLE 4.1   Read three characters

Design an algorithm which will <u>prompt</u> a terminal operator for three characters, <u>accept</u> those characters as input, <u>sort</u> them into ascending sequence and <u>output</u> them to the screen.

A Defining diagram

Input	Processing	Output
char_1	Prompt for characters	char_1
char_2	Accept three characters	char_2
char_3	Sort three characters	char_3
	Output three characters	

B Solution algorithm

The solution algorithm requires a series of IF statements to sort the three characters into ascending sequence.

Read_three_characters

Prompt the operator for char_1, char_2, char_3	
Get char_1, char_2, char_3	

IF char_1 > char_2	
yes	no
temp = char_1 char_1 = char_2 char_2 = temp	

IF char_2 > char_3	
yes	no
temp = char_2 char_2 = char_3 char_3 = temp	

IF char_1 > char_2	
yes	no
temp = char_1 char_1 = char_2 char_2 = temp	

Output to the screen; char_1, char_2, char_3	

EXAMPLE 4.2 *Process customer record*

A program is required to <u>read</u> a customer's name, a purchase amount and a tax code. The tax code has been validated and will be one of the following:

0   tax exempt (0%)
1   state sales tax only (3%)
2   federal and state sales tax (5%)
3   special sales tax (7%)

The program must then <u>compute</u> the sales tax and the total amount due and <u>print</u> the customer's name, purchase amount, sales tax, and total amount due.

A *Defining diagram*

Input	Processing	Output
cust_name	Read customer details	cust_name
purch_amt	Compute sales tax	purch_amt
tax_code	Compute total amount	sales_tax
	Print customer details	total_amt

B   Solution algorithm

The solution algorithm requires a linear nested IF statement to calculate the sales tax.

Process_customer_record

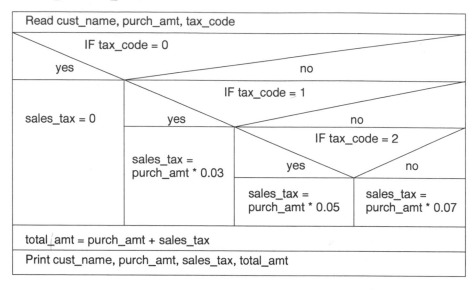

| total_amt = purch_amt + sales_tax |
| Print cust_name, purch_amt, sales_tax, total_amt |

EXAMPLE 4.3   Calculate employee's pay

A program is required by a company to read an employee's number, pay rate and the number of hours worked in a week. The program is then to compute the employee's weekly pay and print it along with the input data.

According to the company's rules, no employee may be paid for more than 60 hours per week, and the maximum hourly rate is $25.00 per hour. If more than 35 hours are worked, then payment for the overtime hours worked is calculated at time-and-a-half. If the hours worked field or the hourly rate field is out of range, then the input data and an appropriate message is to be printed and the employee's weekly pay is not to be calculated.

A   Defining diagram

Input	Processing	Output
emp_no	Read employee details	emp_no
pay_rate	Validate input fields	pay_rate
hrs_worked	Calculate employee pay	hrs_worked
	Print employee details	emp_weekly_pay
		error_message

B Solution algorithm

The solution to this problem will require a series of simple IF and nested IF statements. Firstly, the variables 'pay_rate' and 'hrs_worked' must be validated, and if either is found to be out of range then an appropriate message is to be placed into a variable called 'error_message'.

The employee's weekly pay is only to be calculated if the variables 'pay_rate' and 'hrs_worked' are valid, so another variable 'valid_input_fields' will be used to indicate to the program whether or not these input fields are valid.

The variable 'valid_input_fields' acts as an internal switch or flag to the program. It will initially be set to true, and will be assigned the value false if one of the input fields is found to be invalid. The employee's weekly pay will be calculated only if 'valid_input_fields' is true.

Compute_employee_pay

Set valid_input_fields to true
Set error_message to blank
Read emp_no, pay_rate, hrs_worked

IF pay_rate > $25.00	
yes	no
error_message = 'Pay rate exceeds $25.00' valid_input_fields = false Print emp_no, pay_rate, hrs_worked, error_message	

IF hrs_worked > 60	
yes	no
error_message = 'Hours worked exceeds limit of 60' valid_input_fields = false Print emp_no, pay_rate, hrs_worked, error_message	

IF valid_input_fields		
yes		no
IF hrs_worked ≤ 35		
yes	no	
emp_weekly_pay = pay_rate * hrs_worked	overtime_hrs = hrs_worked − 35 overtime_pay = overtime_hrs * pay_rate * 1.5 emp_weekly_pay = (pay_rate * 35) + overtime_pay	
Print emp_no, pay_rate, hrs_worked, emp_weekly_pay		

THE CASE STRUCTURE EXPRESSED AS AN N-S DIAGRAM

The case control structure is another way of expressing a linear nested IF statement. It is not really an additional control structure; but one which extends the basic selection control structure to be a choice between multiple values. It is expressed as a Nassi-Schneiderman diagram as follows:

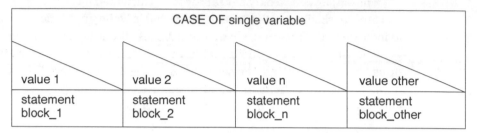

Let us now look again at Example 4.2. The solution algorithm for this example was earlier expressed as a linear nested IF statement, but it could equally have been expressed as a CASE statement.

EXAMPLE 4.4   *Process customer record*

A program is required to <u>read</u> a customer's name, a purchase amount and a tax code. The tax code has been validated and will be one of the following:

0   tax exempt (0%)
1   state sales tax only (3%)
2   federal and state sales tax (5%)
3   special sales tax (7%)

The program is required to <u>compute</u> the sales tax and the total amount due and <u>print</u> the customer's name, purchase amount, sales tax, and total amount due.

A Defining diagram

Input	Processing	Output
cust_name	Read customer details	cust_name
purch_amt	Compute sales tax	purch_amt
tax_code	Compute total amount	sales_tax
	Print customer details	total_amt

B Solution algorithm

The solution algorithm is expressed using a CASE statement:

Process_customer_record

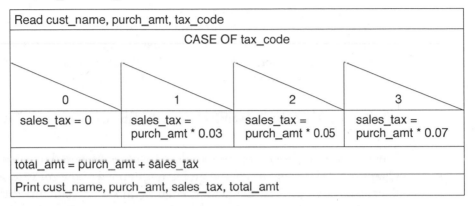

Read cust_name, purch_amt, tax_code			
CASE OF tax_code			
0	1	2	3
sales_tax = 0	sales_tax = purch_amt * 0.03	sales_tax = purch_amt * 0.05	sales_tax = purch_amt * 0.07
total_amt = purch_amt + sales_tax			
Print cust_name, purch_amt, sales_tax, total_amt			

N-S DIAGRAMS AND THE REPETITION CONTROL STRUCTURE

In Chapter 5 the DOWHILE construct was introduced as the pseudocode representation of a repetition loop. This can be represented by an N-S diagram as follows:

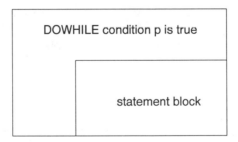

As the DOWHILE loop is a leading decision loop, the following processing takes place:

(a) The logical condition p is tested.
(b) If condition p is found to be true, the statements within the statement block will be executed once. Control will then return to the retesting of condition p (step a).
(c) If condition p is found to be false, control passes to the next statement after the DOWHILE box, and no further processing takes place.

As a result, the DOWHILE structure will continue to repeat a group of statements WHILE a condition remains true. As soon as the condition becomes false, the construct is exited.

There are two important things to consider before designing a DOWHILE loop.

Firstly, the testing of the condition is at the beginning of the loop. This means that you may need to perform some initial processing to adequately set up the condition before it can be tested.

Secondly, the only way to terminate the loop is to render the DOWHILE condition false. This means that you must set up some process within the statement block which will eventually change the condition so that it becomes false. Failure to do this may result in an endless loop.

SIMPLE ALGORITHMS WHICH USE THE REPETITION CONTROL STRUCTURE

The following examples are the same as those represented by pseudocode in Chapter 5. In each example, the problem is defined and a solution algorithm developed using a Nassi-Schneiderman diagram. To help define the problem, the processing verbs in each example have been underlined.

EXAMPLE 5.1 *Fahrenheit–Celsius conversion*

Every day, a weather station receives 15 temperatures expressed in degrees Fahrenheit. A program is to be written which will accept each Fahrenheit temperature, convert it to Celsius and display the converted temperature to the screen. After 15 temperatures have been processed, the words 'All temperatures processed' are to be displayed to the screen.

A *Defining diagram*

Input	Processing	Output
f_temp	Get Fahrenheit temperatures	c_temp
(15 temperatures)	Convert temperatures	(15 temperatures)
	Display Celsius temperatures	
	Display screen message	

The defining diagram still only lists what needs to be done; the equation to convert the temperature will not need to be known until the algorithm is developed.

Having defined the input, output and processing, you should now be ready to outline a solution to the problem. This can be done by writing down the control structures needed and any extra variables which are to be used in the solution algorithm. In this example you will need:

- a DOWHILE structure to repeat the necessary processing, and
- a counter, initialised at zero, which will control the 15 repetitions. This

counter, called temperature_count, will contain the number of temperatures read and processed.

B   Solution algorithm

Fahrenheit_Celsius_conversion

Set temperature_count to zero
DOWHILE temperature_count < 15

Prompt operator for f_temp
      Get f_temp
      Compute c_temp = (f_temp − 32) * 5/9
      Display c_temp
      Add 1 to temperature_count

Display 'All temperatures processed' to the screen

EXAMPLE 5.2   *Print examination scores*

A program is required to read and print a series of names and exam scores for students enrolled in a mathematics course. The class average is to be computed and printed at the end of the report. Scores can range from 0 to 100. The last record contains a blank name and a score of 999 and is not to be included in the calculations.

A   Defining diagram

Input	Processing	Output
name exam_score	Read student details Print student details Compute average score Print average_score	name exam_score average_score

You will need to consider the following requirements when establishing a solution algorithm:

- a DOWHILE structure to control the reading of exam scores, until it reaches a score of 999,
- an accumulator for total scores (total_score), and
- an accumulator for the total students (total_students).

B Solution algorithm

Print_examination_scores

Set total_score to zero
Set total_students to zero
Read name, exam_score

DOWHILE exam_score NOT = 999	
	Add 1 to total_students
	Print name, exam_score
	Add exam_score to total_score
	Read name, exam_score

IF total_students NOT = zero	
yes	no
average_score = total_score / total_students	
Print average_score	

EXAMPLE 5.3 *Process student enrolments*

A program is required which will <u>read</u> a file of student records, and <u>select</u> and <u>print</u> only those students enrolled in a course unit named Programming I. Each student record contains student number, name, address, postcode, gender and course unit number. The course unit number for Programming I is 18500. Three totals are to be <u>printed</u> at the end of the report: total females enrolled in the course; total males enrolled in the course, and total students enrolled in the course.

A Defining diagram

Input	Processing	Output
student_record	Read student records	selected student records
• student_no	Select student records	totals
• name	Print selected records	
• address	Compute total females enrolled	
• postcode	Compute total males enrolled	
• gender	Compute total students enrolled	
• course_unit	Print totals	

You will need to consider the following requirements, when establishing a solution algorithm:

- a DOWHILE structure to perform the repetition,
- an IF statement to select the required students, and
- accumulators for the three total fields.

There is no trailer record for this student file. In cases like this, the terms 'more data', 'more records', 'records exist' or 'not EOF' (end of file) can be used in the DOWHILE condition clause.

B   Solution algorithm

Process_student_enrolments

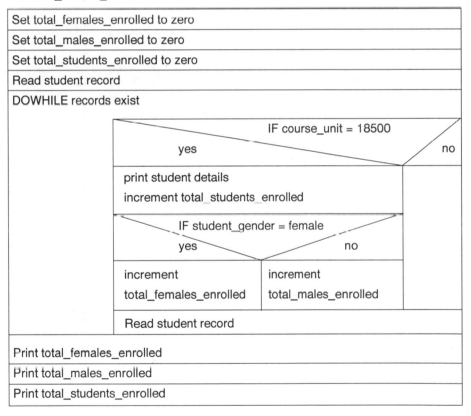

EXAMPLE 5.4   *Process inventory items*

A program is required to <u>read</u> a series of inventory records which contain item number, item description and stock figure. The last record in the file has an item number of zero. The program is to <u>produce</u> a 'Low Stock Items' report, by <u>printing</u> only those records which have a stock figure of less than

20 items. A heading is to be printed at the top of the report and a total low stock item count is to be printed at the end.

A Defining diagram

Input	Processing	Output
inventory record	Read inventory records	heading
• item_number	Select low stock items	selected records
• item_description	Print low stock records	• item_number
• stock_figure	Print total low stock records	• item_description
		• stock_figure
		total_low_stock_items

You will need to consider the following requirements when establishing a solution algorithm:

- a DOWHILE structure to perform the repetition,
- an IF statement to select stock figures of less than 20, and
- an accumulator for total_low_stock_items.

B Solution algorithm

Process_inventory_records

Set total_low_stock_items to zero
Print 'Low Stock Items' heading
Read inventory record
DOWHILE item_number > zero

IF stock_figure < 20

yes / no

Print item_number, item_description, stock_figure
increment total_low_stock_items

Read inventory record

Print total_low_stock_items

S*pecial algorithms*

This appendix contains a number of algorithms which are not included in the body of the book but may be required at some time in your career.

The first section contains three sorting algorithms: bubble sort, insertion sort, and selection sort. The second section contains five algorithms which manipulate the elements of an array. The third section introduces three dynamic data structures (queues, stacks, and linked lists) and provides algorithms to manipulate them.

SORTING ALGORITHMS

Bubble sort algorithm

This algorithm sorts an integer array into ascending order using a bubble sort method.

On each pass, the algorithm compares each pair of adjacent items in the array. If the pair is out of order they are switched, otherwise they remain in the original order. So at the end of the first pass, the largest element in the array will have bubbled to the last position in the array.

The next pass will work only with the remaining elements, and will move the next largest element to the second-last position in the array and so on.

In the algorithm:

Array = array to be sorted

number_of_elements = number of elements in the array

elements_switched = flag to record if the elements have been switched in the current pass

temp = temporary area for holding an array element which is being switched

I = index for outer loop

J = index for inner loop

Assume that the contents of Array and number_of_elements have already been established.

```
Bubble_sort_algorithm
    set I to number_of_elements
    set elements_switched to true
    DOWHILE (elements_switched AND I ≥ 2)
        set J to 1
        set elements_switched to false
        DOWHILE J ≤ I − 1
            IF Array (J) > Array (J + 1) THEN
                temp = Array (J)
```

```
                    Array (J) = Array (J + 1)
                    Array (J + 1) = temp
                    elements_switched = true
                ENDIF
                J = J + 1
            ENDDO
            I = I – 1
        ENDDO
END
```

Insertion sort algorithm

This algorithm sorts an integer array into ascending order using an insertion sort method.

In the algorithm, the array is scanned until an out-of-order element is found. The scan is then temporarily halted while a backward scan is made to find the correct position to insert the out-of-order element. Elements bypassed during this backward scan are moved up one position to make room for the element being inserted.

This method of sorting is more efficient than the bubble sort.

In the algorithm:

Array = array to be sorted

number_of_elements = number of elements in the array

temp = temporary area for holding an array element while correct position is being searched

I = current position of the element

J = index for inner loop

Assume that the contents of Array and number_of_elements have been established.

```
Insertion_sort_algorithm
        set I to 1
        DOWHILE I ≤ (number_of_elements – 1)
            IF Array (I) > Array (I + 1) THEN
                temp = Array (I + 1)
                J – I
                DOWHILE (J ≥ 1 AND Array (J) > temp)
                    Array (J + 1) = Array (J)
                    J = J – 1
                ENDDO
                Array (J + 1) = temp
            ENDIF
            I = I + 1
        ENDDO
    END
```

Selection sort algorithm

This algorithm sorts an integer array into ascending sequence using a selection sort method.

On the first pass the algorithm finds the smallest element in the array and moves it to the first position in the array by switching it with the element originally in that position. Each successive pass moves one more element into position. After the number of passes is one number less than the number of elements in the array, the array will be in order.

In the algorithm:

Array = array being sorted

number_of_elements = number of elements in the array

smallest_element = area for holding the smallest element found in that pass

current_smallest_position = the value of the current position in which to place the smallest element

I = index for outer loop

J = index for inner loop

Assume that the contents of Array and number_of_elements have been established.

```
Selection_sort_algorithm
    Set current_smallest_position to 1
    DOWHILE current_smallest_position ≤ (number_of_elements − 1)
        Set I to current_smallest_position
        smallest_element = Array (I)
        Set J = I + 1
        DOWHILE J ≤ number_of_elements
            IF Array (J) < smallest_element THEN
                I = J
                smallest_element = Array (J)
            ENDIF
            J = J + 1
        ENDDO
        Array (I) = Array (current_smallest_position)
        Array (current_smallest_position) = smallest_element
        Add 1 to current_smallest_position
    ENDDO
END
```

ALGORITHMS WHICH MANIPULATE ARRAYS

The following algorithms involve the manipulation of arrays. Assume that the contents of Array, and number_of_elements have been established.

Find the sum of the elements of an array

```
Calculate_sum_of_elements
     set sum to zero
     set I to 1
     DOWHILE I ≤ number_of_elements
         sum = sum + Array(I)
         I = I + 1
     ENDDO
     Print sum
END
```

Find the largest of the elements of an array

```
Find_largest_element
     set I to 1
     set largest_element to Array(1)
     DOWHILE I < number_of_elements
         IF Array(I + 1) > largest_element THEN
             largest_element = Array(I + 1)
         ENDIF
         I = I + 1
     ENDDO
     Print largest_element
END
```

Find the smallest of the elements of an array

```
Find_smallest_element
     set I to 1
     set smallest_element to Array(1)
     DOWHILE I < number_of_elements
         IF Array(I + 1) < smallest_element THEN
             smallest_element = Array(I + 1)
         ENDIF
         I = I + 1
     ENDDO
     Print smallest_element
END
```

Find the range of the elements of an array

```
Find_range_of_elements
     set I to 1
     set smallest_element to Array(1)
     set largest_element to Array(1)
     DOWHILE I < number_of_elements
         IF Array(I + 1) < smallest_element THEN
             smallest_element = Array(I + 1)
         ELSE
```

```
            IF Array(I + 1) > largest_element THEN
                largest_element = Array(I + 1)
            ENDIF
        ENDIF
        I = I + 1
    ENDDO
    Print the range as smallest_element followed by largest_element
END
```

Find the mean of the elements of an array

```
Find_mean_of_elements
    set I to 1
    set sum to zero
    DOWHILE I ≤ number_of_elements
        sum = sum + Array(I)
        I = I + 1
    ENDDO
    mean = sum / number_of_elements
    Print mean
END
```

DYNAMIC DATA STRUCTURES

An array is called a static data structure because in common programming languages the maximum number of elements must be specified when the array is declared. A dynamic data structure is one in which the number of elements can expand or contract as the problem requires. The elements in these data structures are called nodes.

In building dynamic data structures, pointers are used to create new nodes, and link nodes dispose of those no longer needed. A pointer is a variable whose memory cell contains the address in memory where a data item resides. Therefore, a pointer provides an indirect reference to a data item.

This section covers several examples of dynamic data structures, including queues, stacks and linked lists. Algorithms which manipulate these structures are also provided.

Queues

A queue is a data structure holding data items which are processed on a first-in-first-out basis, like a line of people going through a cafeteria: the first one in the line is the first to reach the cash register and get out of the line.

There are two operations which can be performed on a queue: a node can be added to the end of a queue, and a node can be removed from the head of a queue.

Some programming languages do not support the notion of dynamic data structures, and so do not provide a pointer type. In such cases, the easiest way of representing a queue in an algorithm is by declaring it to be an array. The effect of a pointer is then achieved by using an integer variable to hold the subscript of the array element representing the node which is currently being operated on. Pointers are required to locate the position of the head of the queue and the tail of the queue, as these must be known. Most queues are designed so that the head of the queue wraps around to the tail when required.

Names used in the algorithms are:

Queue = queue to be manipulated
max_size = maximum number of items in the queue
queue_counter = current number of items in the queue
queue_head = position of the head of the queue
queue_tail = position at which the next item will be inserted in the queue.

The pseudocode to add an item and to delete an item from a queue are:

```
Add_item_to_tail_of_queue
    IF (queue_tail = queue_head AND queue_counter > 0)
        Print error message ('queue overflow')
    ELSE
        Queue (queue_tail) = new item
        queue_tail = queue_tail + 1
        IF queue_tail > max_size THEN
            queue_tail = 1
        ENDIF
        queue_counter = queue_counter + 1
    ENDIF
END
```

```
Remove_item_from_head_of_queue
    IF queue_counter = 0 THEN
        Print error message ('queue is empty')
    ELSE
        required value = Queue (queue_head)
        queue_head = queue_head + 1
        IF queue_head > max_size THEN
            queue_head = 1
            ENDIF
        queue_counter = queue_counter − 1
    ENDIF
END
```

It is not necessary to alter the data item that is 'removed' from the queue, because it will simply be overwritten if its place is required.

Stacks

A stack is a data structure holding data items which are processed in a last-in-first-out basis, like a stack of trays in a cafeteria: when a tray is required, it is removed from the top of the stack, and when one is added to the stack, it is also placed on the top. These operations on stack data structures are often called 'pop' (for removing the top element) and 'push' (for adding a new element to the stack).

Once again, the easiest way of representing this stack in an algorithm is by declaring it to be an array.

```
In the algorithms:
Stack = stack to be manipulated;
max_size = the maximum size of the stack;
top_of_stack = the position of the top of the stack.


Add_item_to_top_of_stack  (Push)
    IF top_of_stack NOT = max_size THEN
        top_of_stack = top_of_stack + 1
        Stack (top_of_stack) = new item
    ELSE
        Print error message ('stack overflow')
    ENDIF
END

Remove_item_from_top_of_stack  (Pop)
    IF top_of_stack NOT = zero THEN
        value required = Stack (top_of_stack)
        top_of_stack = top_of_stack − 1
    ELSE
        Print error message ('stack underflow')
    ENDIF
END
```

Once again, it is not necessary to alter the the data item that is 'removed' from the stack, as it will be over-written when the next item is added.

Linked lists

A (linear) linked list is a data structure holding a series of elements or cells which contain both a data item and a pointer to the next element in the list. A linked list can be illustrated as follows:

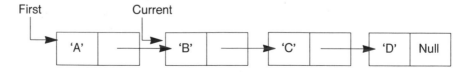

In the above diagram the pointer called 'First' points to the first cell in the list and the pointer called 'Current' points to the current cell in the list. The pointer in the last cell is labelled 'Null', as it indicates the end of the list. Null does not point to a data value.

The advantage of such a data structure is that the elements in the list may be added or deleted by manipulating the pointers rather than by physically moving the data. The data structure thus can be maintained in a logical sequence, without that logical sequence being physically implemented.

Again, where the programming language does not support a pointer type, the easiest way of representing a linked list is by using a technique of 'parallel arrays'. Here, one array holds the items in the list and the other array holds, at corresponding positions, the 'link' to the (logically) next item, i.e. the value of the subscript of the next item. An integer variable is needed to hold the subscript of the 'first' item (in logical order), and some convention must be adopted whereby an impossible subscript value is understood to be a Null pointer.

Names used in the algorithms are:

Items = an array holding the list values;

Links = an array holding subscripts of the next items;

first = the subscript of the first item in the list;

current = the subscript of the list item currently being operated on;

last = the subscript of the the 'previous' item to the 'current' item;

continue = a Boolean variable set to true to indicate that the search for
a value is to continue.

Pseudocode examples which manipulate a singly linked linear list follow:

1   Traverse a list, printing its value

```
Traverse_and_print
    current = first
    DOWHILE current NOT = Null
        Print Items (current)
        current = Links (current)
    ENDDO
END
```

2   Search a list for a particular value ('value')

```
Search_list_for_value
    current = first
    continue = true
    DOWHILE (continue AND current NOT = Null)
        IF items (current) NOT = value THEN
            last = current
            current = Links (current)
        ELSE
            continue = false
```

```
            ENDIF
        ENDDO
    END
```

Note that continue will still be true if the value was not in the list, in which case current will be Null.

3   Remove a designated value from the list. (This algorithm follows on from the one above, where the value was located.)

```
Remove_value_from_list
    IF NOT continue THEN (i.e. the value was found on the list)
        IF current = first THEN
            first = Links (current)
        ELSE
            Links (last) = Links (current)
        ENDIF
    ENDIF
END
```

In practice, the position of the space just freed would be recorded for later use. This would require the definition of an integer variable 'free' to hold the subscript of the first element of free space. Then after a remove operation the free list would be updated with the statements:

Links (current) = free
free = current

More complex linked structures such as binary trees and graphs and the algorithms to manipulate them are beyond the present scope of this book. They may be found in more advanced programming texts and introductory Computer Science texts.

Glossary

algorithm
A set of detailed, unambiguous and ordered instructions developed to describe the processes necessary to produce the desired output from a given input.

array
A data structure made up of a number of data items which all have the same type and are accessed by the same name.

Boolean variable
A variable which can contain only one of two possible values; true or false.

CASE control structure
A structure which extends the basic selection control structure from a choice between two values to a choice from multiple values.

cohesion
A measure of the internal strength of a module, i.e. how closely the elements or statements of a module are associated with each other. The higher the cohesion, the better the module.

constant
A data item with a name and a value which remains the same during the execution of a program.

control structures
The Structure Theorem states that it is possible to write any program using only three basic control structures:
(i) sequence: the straightforward execution of one processing step after another.
(ii) selection: the presentation of a condition, and the choice between two actions, depending on whether the condition is true or false.

(iii) repetition: the presentation of a set of instructions to be performed repeatedly, as long as a condition is true.

coupling
A measure of the extent of information interchange between modules. The fewer the connections between modules, the more loosely they are coupled. The looser the coupling, the better the module.

data structure
A collection of elementary data items.

data type
A set of values and a set of operations which can be performed on those values.

defining diagram
A diagram which arranges the input, output and processing components of a problem into separate columns. It is constructed when the programmer defines the problem.

dynamic data structure
One in which the number of elements can expand or contract as the problem requires.

elementary data item
One which contains a single variable that is always treated as a unit.

file
A collection of related records.

functional decomposition
The division of a problem into separate tasks or functions as the first step towards designing the solution algorithm. Each function will be dedicated to the performance of a single specific task.

global data
Data which is known to the whole world of the program.

hierarchy chart
A diagram which shows the name of each module in the solution algorithm and its hierarchical relationship to the other modules.

information hiding
A concept used in object-oriented design methodology where the structure of the data is hidden from the user.

inter-module communication
The flow of information or data between modules.

linked list
A data structure which holds a series of elements which contain both a data item and a pointer to the next item in the list.

literal
A constant whose name is the written representation of its value.

local data
Data which is defined within the module in which it is referenced and is not known outside that module.

mainline
The controlling module of a solution algorithm which ties all the modules together and co-ordinates their activity.

modular design
Grouping tasks together because they all perform the same function. Modular design is directly connected to top-down development, as the tasks into which you divide the problem form the future modules of the program.

module
A section of an algorithm dedicated to the performance of a single task.

object
A region of memory in which the values of a given data type are stored.

object-oriented design
A methodology which views the system as a collection of interacting objects whose internal structure is hidden from the user

parameter
A variable, literal or constant which is used to communicate between the modules of a program.
- Data parameters contain the actual variables or data items which will be passed between modules.
- Status parameters act as program flags and should contain just one of two values, true or false.

pointer
A variable whose memory cell contains the address in memory where a data item resides.

priming Read
A statement which appears immediately before the DOWHILE condition in a solution algorithm.

pseudocode
A subset of English which has been formalised and abbreviated to look like a high level computer language. Keywords and indentation are used to signify particular control structures.

queue
A data structure holding data items which are processed on a first-in-first-out basis.

record
A collection of data items or fields which all bear some relationship to each other.

scope of a variable
The portion of a program in which a variable has been defined and can be referred to; i.e. a list of all the modules in which that variable can be referenced.

sentinel
A special record placed at the end of valid data to signify the end of that data. It is also known as a trailer record.

side effect
This occurs when a subordinate module alters the value of a global variable.

stack
A data structure holding data items which are processed on a last-in-first-out basis.

string
A collection of characters.

Structure Theorem
The Structure Theorem states that it is possible to write any computer program by using only three basic control structures. These control structures are simple sequence, selection and repetition.

structured programming
A method of writing programs so that each instruction obeys the Structure Theorem. Structured programming also incorporates top-down development and modular design.

top-down development
The division of a problem into separate tasks as the first step towards designing the solution algorithm. The programmer develops an algorithm which incorporates the major tasks first, and only considers the more detailed steps when all the major tasks have been completed.

variable
A collection of memory cells which store a particular data item.

Index

Note: bold numbers indicate the primary reference for entries with more than one reference.